LEO BUSCAGLIA

LOVING
EACH OTHER

THE CHALLENGE OF HUMAN RELATIONSHIPS

Other Books by the author

The Fall of Freddie the Leaf

Living, Loving & Learning

The Disabled and Their Parents:
A Counseling Challenge

Personhood

The Way of the Bull

Because I am Human

Love

Library of Congress catalog number: LC-84-50590
SLACK Incorporated ISBN: 0-943432-27-8
Holt, Rinehart and Winston ISBN: 0-03-000083-1

Published in the United States of America by
SLACK Incorporated
6900 Grove Road
Thorofare, New Jersey 08086

In the United States, Distributed to the trade by:
Holt, Rinehart and Winston
383 Madison Avenue
New York, New York 10017

In Canada, distributed by:
Holt, Rinehart and Winston, Limited
55 Horner Avenue
Toronto, Ontario
M8Z 4X0 Canada

Printed in the United States of America

This book is dedicated to my family: Vincent, Margie, Lee, Annie, Frank and Pete; and to Tulio and Rosa who started it all.

It is also dedicated to those who helped me put it together: Steven, Norma, Gary and Becky, Barbara, Charles and Peter. I am indebted, also, to the over 600 individuals who took the time to answer a long and rather complicated questionnaire in order to share their personal experiences and thoughts about loving relationships.

I love you all!

Leo

We are each of us angels with only one wing. And we can only fly embracing each other.

— LUCIANO DE CRESCENZO

TABLE OF CONTENTS

A FOREWORD, A PREAMBLE, AND A MYTH

FOREWORD

Why are we so afraid to commit ourselves to loving each other?

This is a book about love, tenderness, compassion, caring, sharing, and relating — the most vital of human behaviors. Without these qualities life is empty though we may have the best of health, the most comfortable of homes, the most impressive of bank balances. Even knowing this, we spend so little time developing these behaviors. In fact, we are living in a society in which such words as love and commitment have been relegated to sentimental, old-fashioned nonsense. Skeptics are only too ready and capable with quick wit and stinging phrases to ridicule those who continue to speak of broken hearts, of devastating loneliness and the mystical ways and power of love.

If you love, you are considered naive. If happy, you are considered frivolous and simple. If generous and altruistic, you are considered suspect. If forgiving, you are considered weak. If trusting, you are considered a fool. If you try to be all of these things, people are sure you are phony. This flippant attitude has had much to do with the breeding of a society of detached, noncommitted persons too sophisticated to admit to their confusion and unhappiness and too caught up in ego to risk doing anything about it. It has perpetuated isolation and devalued basic human values. This, in spite of the fact that over the past years there has been amassed a vast scientific literature which proves that relationships *do* matter, that intimacy *is* necessary to sustain a good, productive life, that a loving touch or a hearty laugh *can* heal, that positive relating *brings* physical, psychological and mental well being. Such contemporary philosophers and scientists as Ashley Montagu, Carl Rogers, A.H. Maslow, Harold Bloomfield, Elizabeth Kübler Ross, Desmond Morris, James Lynch, Theodore Isaac Rubin, Margaret Mead, Norman Cousins, David Viscott, Clark Moustakas, William Menninger, Melanie Klein, C.S. Lewis, Nathaniel Branden and others have persisted in their writings and research, in spite of their critics, in affirming that a society devoid of these basic human needs is doomed.

Our growing inability to relate one with another is reaching frightening proportions. Soon the two-parent family will be considered the exception. Notions of marriage, of extended families and long-lasting friendships are more and more being considered outmoded. Meaningless sexual promiscuity is accepted as the norm and even being advocated as useful behavior for solving problems in failing marriages. Emotional detachment, maintaining our distance from others, is being prescribed as a solution for avoiding pain. Neglect and abuse of children and the aged is a growing problem. Social and religious institutions, which in the past helped to set standards of behavior and brought people together in companionship, are actively downgraded. Individualism, independence and personal freedom are valued above love, commitment, and cooperation.

Examining the complex nature involved in loving each other (the dynamic and everchanging nature of two or more unique and whole individuals agreeing to emerge and blend in long-term commitment) is not an easy task. Nevertheless, that is the purpose of this book. It seems to me vital and necessary, since material dealing with the dynamics of loving each other is rare. Without this knowledge we end only by living together in hate, fear, loneliness, and continuing to hurt each other in ignorance. Happily, the choice is still ours to make.

Like everyone I know, my life, too, has been a long series of interwoven relationships, both good and bad. I value them all. For it was mainly through these relationships that I survived my infancy, completed my childhood, ended my adolescence and moved toward a dynamic state of growing to maturity. They have been living lessons in meeting defeat, letting go and overcoming fear. They have helped to free my spirit and irradicate my fear of loving. My relationships are still my major source of stimulation, causing me to remain open, curious, eager to learn and challenged by change. Now I understand more than ever the poet W.H. Auden's remark, "We must love one another or die!"

Isn't it time that we forget our petty egos, give up our fear of appearing sentimental or naive and come together in our universal need, one for the other? Why is it so difficult for us to embrace each other fearlessly and with passion and to say, "Human being, take my human hand"?

There is a wonderful fable that tells of a young girl who is walking through a meadow when she sees a butterfly impaled upon a thorn. Very carefully she releases it and the butterfly starts to fly away. Then it comes back and changes into a beautiful good fairy. "For your kindness," she tells the little girl, "I will grant you your fondest wish." The little girl thinks for a moment and replies, "I want to be happy." The fairy leans toward her and whispers in her ear and then suddenly vanishes.

As the girl grew, no one in the land was more happy than she. Whenever anyone asked her for the secret of her happiness, she would only smile and say, "I listened to a good fairy."

As she grew quite old, the neighbors were afraid the fabulous secret might die with her. "Tell us, please," they begged, "tell us what the fairy said." The now lovely old lady simply smiled and said, "She told me that everyone, no matter how secure they seemed, had need of me!"

We all need each other.

PREAMBLE

There comes a time in some relationships when no matter how sincere the attempt to reconcile the differences or how strong the wish to recreate a part of the past once shared, the struggle becomes so painful that nothing else is felt and the world and all its beauty only add to the discomfort by providing cruel contrast.

DAVID VISCOTT

We are not evil, inadequate or incompetent when our relationships fail. It may have been that we were simply overconfident about them, not adequately prepared for them or unrealistic in our expectations of them. Not all relationships are right. As long as values change, insights expand, human facades remain impenetrable and human behaviors unpredictable, we will make mistakes.

The very measure of a good relationship is in how much it encourages optimal intellectual, emotional and spiritual growth. So, if a relationship becomes destructive, endangers our human dignity, prevents us from growing, continually depresses and demoralizes us — and we have done everything we can to prevent its failure — then, unless we are masochists and enjoy misery, we must eventually terminate it. We are not for everyone and everyone is not for us. The question is, "If we cannot be with another, can we at least not hurt them? Can we, at least, find a way to coexist?"

THE MYTH

We have been poisoned by fairy tales.
ANAÏS NIN

Fallen myths can distill venom.
DENIS DE ROUGEMONT

"And they lived happily ever after."

So goes the eternal myth of loving each other. The fantasy that being in love and forming relationships based upon love will solve all of life's problems and provide us with deserved instant and lasting happiness. The myth is delightful. The reality is too often fierce. But we love to believe in fairy tales. "And they lived happily ever after," says Joshua Liebman, "is one of the most tragic sentences in literature. It is tragic because it tells a falsehood about life and has led countless generations of people to expect something from human existence which is not possible on this fragile, failing, imperfect earth."

I recall being extremely moved watching an interview on public television between interviewer John Callaway and actress Helen Hayes. At age 82, Ms. Hayes looked radiant in the garden of her New York home. She sat proudly in her chair, her face full of the strength which comes from living life fully and with dignity. Mr. Callaway repeatedly asked her very personal questions. None caused her to lose her composure until, alluding to her stormy marriage to writer Charles MacArthur, he suggested that she had never known a totally happy day.

She looked him directly in the eyes and with great dignity responded something to the effect of, "Perhaps not a completely happy day . . . but I knew moments of great ecstasy."

Like Ms. Hayes, many of us have known happy and joyous moments in our relationships. Perhaps a few of us have even known some moments of ecstasy. But those moments have too often been punctuated by times of loneliness, confusion, disappointment and perhaps even despair. In fact, those who appear to have succeeded in having come to terms with life have seemed to expect little more. As Anne Morrow Lindbergh has written:

> When you love someone you do not love them all the time, in exactly the same way, from moment to moment. It is an impossibility. It is even a lie to pretend to. And yet this is exactly what most of us demand. We have so little faith in the ebb and flow of life, of love, of relationships. We leap at the flow of the tide and resist in terror its ebb. We are afraid it will never return. We insist on permanency, on duration, on continuity; when the only continuity possible, in life as in love, is in growth, in fluidity — in freedom.

This is not an easy task. Learning to live with and love others requires skills as delicate and studied as those of the surgeon, the master builder and the gourmet cook, none of whom would dream of practicing each profession without first acquiring the necessary knowledge. Still, we fragile, ill-equipped humans plow ahead, forming friendships, marrying, raising families with few or no actual resources at hand to meet the overwhelming demands. It is no surprise, therefore, that relationships which often begin with joyous wide-eyed naiveté too often end in disillusionment, bitterness and despair. The initial aura of magic seems to fade somewhere in the day-to-night processes of existence. We have all experienced the feeling of being totally captivated and enamored by strangers, who, after a few weeks of relationship, cause us to wonder what we ever saw in them. This fact can be reinforced by noting the skyrocketing divorce rate. As of January 1983, one out of every two marriages ended in divorce. According to the Census Bureau, one-third of our nation's children presently live in homes with one biological parent absent. Even totally surrounded by people, depression based upon feelings of isolation and loneliness is presently the great national malady. Suicide rates are on the increase among the young as well as the aged. Still it never occurs to us to ask why, to research and analyze this threatening situation and find solutions which could guide us to more peaceful and lasting relationships.

A woman from Vermont wrote me that her marriage of 18 years had become a hoax, empty, and not worth continuing. "I haven't anything more to give," she said. "I'm worn out. I feel used. I hate the past 18 years. They seem so meaningless now. I despise what we had. Our years together have led us nowhere, taken everything, and left me nothing. What a useless waste!" A gentleman from Texas wrote, "I don't know what happened. I certainly loved her enough when we were married. At the beginning I thought of her all day long. Over the years, I started getting bored. There are no more surprises. We didn't seem to have much fun anymore and each year we have less in common. I don't like being with her. I don't look forward to coming home. There are long stretches during the day when I forget her altogether. And these become longer each year. It is only when the day is over and I have to go home that she comes to mind."

An elderly woman at one of my lectures told me, "I don't have any friends anymore. I don't know where they've all gone. I don't know what to do. All I know is that I don't seem to have anyone I can talk with. No one asks me out or writes me a letter. No one seems to want or need my company. I've outlived all of my friends. What's left of my family is spread all over the country. I'm afraid to be alone."

Recently, in a Los Angeles newspaper there was an advertisement promoting an agency which offered to send out, at a few moments notice, a "friend." This "friend" would be willing to sit with you, talk with you, or hold your hand if you were ailing and dying. This friend, of course, was only yours as long as you could continue to pay.

I learned of an invalid woman, very much alone, who, in order to keep human contact alive, dialed "Information" and "Time" on her telephone during intervals in her day. "At least it's a human voice talking to me," she said. Now, even the voice of Time is computerized, and Information encourages you not to bother them unless necessary.

"Regulars" on talk shows have been known to wait for hours for a few moments of discussion with the talk show host, no matter how hurried or brief the encounter will be. There are some homes or apartments where the television is never turned off. "It's company."

So many of the letters I receive deal with the pain of isolation, the joylessness and meaninglessness of a life without others in it.

The common theme is, "How can I form relationships and keep them growing and loving?"

A True Story of Loving Each Other

In 1888, Papa was born in a small village in the Italian-Swiss Alps. The village was so small that when, years later, I went back to visit relatives still living there, I could not find it on the Automobile Association map of Italy.

Mama was born in a larger town, just a few miles from Papa's. She was born in the same year, just a month earlier. At the time they were growing up, this region of Italy, the Piemonte, was mostly an area of rolling hills covered with vineyards, red brick farmhouses and scattered small villages, each populated with just a few hundred people. My mother's town actually boasted a "castle," or what appeared to them to be a castle, but which was actually a large villa lived in by "Il Padrone," the owner of the town's only factory. Though Olivetti and Fiat have moved in over the years and changed the environment and the economy of the area, the villages have not changed too much. My remaining relatives are still living in the family homes in which Tulio and Rosa, my parents, were born. But now they have electric lights and indoor plumbing, and their windows, once open, are screened against the onslaught of summer flies and mosquitos.

Neither Mama nor Papa had more than an elementary school education, but interestingly enough this seemed to suffice for them to have become avid readers, deeply reverent about learning and education. Mama could quote from D'Annuncio and Dante. Her favorite novel was Manzoni's classic, *I Promessi Sposi* (The Betrothed), from which she often quoted. She loved opera, especially Puccini, and Mimi was her favorite role. She hummed the luscious arias incessantly. They were, in fact, my lullabies. Mama had long, thick, chestnut hair that grew down to the small of her back. She wore it in a bundle on the back of her head, a braided knot held in place with long Spanish shell pins. A very small person, she had large, deep-set eyes, which, I seem to remember, were always tearing with joy or sorrow. She was exceedingly beautiful. She laughed often and loved eating. Her passions were Tulio (her husband), food, candy and children. (Not necessarily in that order.)

Papa was a tall, handsome man with jet black hair, dark eyes, a light complexion and the most astounding curled moustache in the area. He worked hard all of his life, and though he shared a great deal of love and warmth, financially he just managed to maintain us above the poverty level. He had a way of becoming the scapegoat of bankruptcies, selfish "friends" and poor investments.

There was a mill in Mama's town in which most of the villagers worked. Mama was no exception; she was a spinner. Papa was her foreman. Their marriage was an arranged one. Though they were together at work six days a week, Mama — always very shy — never dared look at Papa. It being a man's world, Papa was free to look at Mama, of course. He was responsible for setting up the processes necessary to bring about their marriage. This he did through the family elders. When both families agreed, Papa was invited to Mama's house for dinners and outings. Mama was present, but never alone with Papa. When Papa visited, she cooked, served, and cleaned but there was no other contact. Even during this period she was too shy to look up and see this man who had chosen to be her husband. The other girls at the factory assured her that he was very handsome, but she did not take her first *real* look at him (so she recalled) until the day of the wedding. She felt she had done well!

Papa was not an adventurer, but knew that there must be more to life than the day-to-day factory work, poverty and hunger. The word had spread even to Piemonte that America was the land of promise and, like so many at the time, he made the decision to sail there one day. It always amazes me that but for that decision, I would still be in the Piemonte area, perhaps working in a factory or growing the grapes for the famous Pasito wine.

Tulio and Rosina had their first child, Vincenzio, in Italy. It was after this that Papa had the opportunity to realize his dream and immigrate to America. It was 1908. Their other natural children, Margarita, Carolina and Felice, were born in the United States. Altogether, they raised eight children (Mama took in children like Papa took in stray cats and dogs).

Papa and Mama stayed married for 63 years. In 1970, Mama was the first to die. Papa died three years later. He was 82. Romantic? Happily ever after? Perhaps not completely — but good enough! What is mentioned above are simply the statistics. What really matters is they laughed a lot, but I also saw them cry. They had great fun together. I saw them overcome times of dire poverty and depression, but I also saw them triumph. I heard them argue and often shout at each other. I watched them exhibit tenderness, an abundance of caring, sharing and love. Never once, though, did I ever hear or see them, in word or action, question being together. "Divorce?" Mama said, "Never! Murder, often! Divorce never!" Though I did not know it at the time, they were showing me the realistic workings of a loving human relationship. They were enhancing the union into which I was welcomed and from which I was to gain my strength: a union in which I, my other family members, and their families and friends, belonged. They were modeling my first loving relationship.

Overcoming the Myth

There is no being or becoming without relationship. From the beginning, we grow to sense the need and import of relatedness. We human beings have the longest period of dependency of any living creature. At birth, in total helplessness, we engage in our first coupling, mother-child, and from that time on, the more sophisticated our lives become, the more interrelated we become. In a sense, we spend our entire existence weaving one relationship into another until we've created, like the web of a spider, a complete pattern.

Our very survival seems to depend upon our relationships. In childhood, if we are denied loving encounters with human beings, we wither, fall into psychosis, idiocy, or die. As adults we continue to depend upon our interactions in togetherness for our greater joys and our most significant growth. We take this process for granted. It seems to be only in moments when we experience disconnection, times when we are severed from close relationships — either by death, divorce, or physical separations that tear our closeness apart and leave us alone — that it becomes apparent. It is strange, then, that even knowing of our desperate need for relating, we continue through much of our lives to engage in thoughtless, vacuous behavior which only results in isolating us further.

Like most of us, my life has been spent in trying to understand and form lasting relationships and in watching those I love attempt to do the same. There are times when I have succeeded. So many of the people with whom I have grown up, family members and long-lasting friends, are still vital parts of my life. There are times when I have failed. I think back fondly and plaintively of the many individuals I have encountered in the past with whom I have shared days, months, even years of extreme joy, but whom I no longer see. Where are they? What are they doing, thinking? Why could I not seem to keep them in my life? Happily, these were few in number. Was it easier then, or harder? I can remember the neighborhood in East Los Angeles in which I lived and grew to adulthood. I remember the family across the street who afforded us so many children from which we could select friends. I recall the boy next door, the rabbi's son, and how close we became. It seems — or was I imagining it — that there was so much more stability, so much less moving about. We found possible relationships in church, in school, at the playground, which remained constant year after year. They formed the permanent network of contacts from which we received our security and strength. They knew our names and we knew theirs. They were part of our great family from which we received our growing identity.

Allan Fromme, in his book, *The Ability to Love*, describes this comfortable, fast-vanishing time. He says:

> Our cities with their swollen populations and cliff dwelling high-rise buildings are breeding places for loneliness. Neighborhoods crumble under the housing development bulldozers and families scatter in pursuit of jobs and professions everywhere. In a world of wheels, old and comfortable groupings of people have disappeared.

Even our daily shopping once afforded us opportunities for relating. We had no super-efficient, one-stop, sterile markets. The butcher down the street who ordered the white milk-fed veal which Mama lovingly made into so many savory dishes, knew each of us. The vegetable stand owner gave us discarded greens for our rabbits. The deli manager who cut the salami, prosciutto, mortadella and cheeses to order, was a family friend. Today forty million people a year change residence in the United States. They move into impersonal cities where people pride themselves in having achieved privacy in that they don't even know their neighbors. They are fearful that others may invade their world and at the same time hope that some of them will.

I recently read of a young man in his mid-twenties who was found dead in his apartment off the campus of the University of Miami, where he was a student. It was reported that he was last seen prior to Thanksgiving. When they found him he had been dead for two months. He hadn't even been missed by anyone at Christmas. On his apartment door were two eviction notices and his television set was still on.

We don't dare to stroll our forbidding sidewalks. Security today has come to mean elaborate alarm systems, armed guards and high-rise housing where we can enter and leave in an elevator which delivers us directly into our living room, assuring us of not one — good or bad — human encounter. More and more opportunities for personal contacts are being taken from us and the chances of forming lasting relationships are becoming significantly more difficult. Some of us have friends whom we care about and see daily in our working environment; but in a city like Los Angeles, for example, it is conceivable that they live as many as thirty miles away. How are we expected to form meaningful relationships when opportunities are so very difficult? Though some of us give lip service to the horror of this "community apathy," we seldom do anything about it. Rather we spend our time elaborating upon feelings of emptiness, alienation, isolation, deprivation, and damn the unfriendliness and indifference of those about us and the society which perpetuates this.

Loving relationships, though necessary for life, health, and growth, are among the most complicated skills. Before we can be successful at achieving relationships, it is necessary that we broaden our understanding of how they work, what they mean and how what we do and believe can enhance or destroy them. We can accomplish this only if we are willing to put in the energy and take the time to study failed relationships as well as examine successful ones. Loving relationships cannot be taken lightly. Unless we are looking for pain, they must not be forever approached in a trial-and-error fashion. Too many of us have experienced the cost of these lackadaisical approaches in terms of tears, confusion and guilt. Referring specifically to married relationships, Carl Rogers stated:

> . . . . . though modern Marriage is a tremendous laboratory, its members are often utterly without preparation for the partnership function. How much agony and remorse and failure could have been avoided if there had been at least some rudimentary learning before they entered the partnership.

And this statement is equally valid for *all* relationships.

THE STUDY

Man is but a network of relationships and these alone matter to him.

ST. EXUPÉRY

These things I command you, that ye love one another.

JOHN 15:17

Studies, both formal and informal, which have been conducted on human relationships over the past years have merely served to enhance my belief in the complexity, mystery and comedy of human behavior. We are so funny. We continue to be the great enigma, so unpredictable, so vulnerable, so wonderful and unique. For example, most studies concur that security, joy and success in life are directly correlated to our ability to relate, one with the other, with some degree of commitment, depth and love. We have learned, most of us from experience, that our inability to live in harmony with others is responsible for our greatest fears, anxieties, feelings of isolation and even severe mental illness. Still, even after many painful failures, precious few of us have deliberately sought information to clarify and ameliorate our dilemma. Even those of us who hunger for closeness and more understanding discover in our search that there are few places to which we can turn for help.

There is an amusing story of a young man who decides he wants to learn how to better relate to others. He goes to a bookstore and is hard pressed to find anything to help him. He finally comes upon a book that seems helpful. It is titled, "How to Hug." When he returns home he finds that he has bought Volume Nine of an encyclopedia!

Unable to find help, we generally continue to engage blindly in painful, unfulfilling relationships which by their very nature sap us of our energies and delay our growth. We find that we lack the strength, the knowledge and the creativity to meet the subtle, complex demands of relating. Even after centuries of human interacting, children still continue to rebel against their parents and siblings. Young marrieds look upon their in-laws and parents as obstacles to their independence and growth. Parents view their children as selfish ingrates. Husbands desert their wives and seek greener fields elsewhere. Wives form relationships with heroes of soap operas who vicariously bring excitement and romance into their empty lives. Workers often hate their bosses and co-workers and spend miserable hours with them, day after day. On a larger scale, management cannot relate with labor. Each accuses the other of unreasonable self-interests and narrow-mindedness. Religious groups often become entrapped, each in a provincial dogma resulting in hate and vindictiveness in the name of God. Nations battle blindly, under the shadow of world annihilation, for the realization of their personal rights. Members of these groups blame rival groups for their continual sense of frustration, impotence, lack of progress and communication.

We have obviously not learned much over the years. We have not paused long enough to consider the simple truth that we humans are not born with particular attitudinal sets regarding other persons, we are taught into them. We are the future generation's teachers. We are, therefore, the perpetuators of the confusion and alienation we abhor and which keep us impotent in finding new alternatives. It is up to us to diligently discover new solutions and learn new patterns of relating, ways more conducive to growth, peace, hope and loving coexistence. Anything that is learned can be unlearned and relearned. In this process called *change* lies our real hope.

For years I have been frustrated with the lack of concern regarding relationships. A few years ago I decided to do something about it. I commenced to conduct studies among the architects of relationships themselves. How better to learn about successes and failures in relating than from those actively engaged in the daily struggle of living together in peace and love? In this way I hoped to shed some light on how we may better accept the challenge and commitment of loving each other.

I sent out a rather extensive questionnaire, offering an opportunity to contribute to the subject of relationships. It contained both closed- and open-ended questions so that the respondents would be specific as well as feel free to elaborate on their answers. For the purpose of the study, the formal definition of a relationship was:

> "a socially sanctioned, enduring, mutually-agreed-upon connection or union, which fulfills certain needs of the individuals involved and the society in which they live."

After the usual demographic information, the questions asked related to two areas:

1. A primary relationship defined as the clos-

31

est person with whom you presently choose to relate, or are forced to do so, on a regular basis in your daily life.

2. A secondary relationship defined as the person you choose to relate with, or are forced to do so, on a regular basis, but with a lesser degree of intensity and day-to-day encounter than your primary relationship.

The respondents were then asked to name the qualities which they felt were most conducive to maintaining a loving, growing relationship, and those qualities which were the most destructive to a loving relationship. In addition, each was asked to define a loving relationship and to offer any advice they would give to those engaged in the process of forming lasting relationships.

One thousand questionnaires were mailed at random to men and women who had written to me at one time or another indicating their interest in the dynamics of loving relationships. Astoundingly, there was more than an enthusiastic 60 percent return, indicating the keen interest in the subject.

Before entering into an analysis of the results, it might be interesting at this point if you, the reader, would conduct your own personal survey. There is much to be learned about yourself, your needs and your expectations by answering the same questions. The questions on the next two pages are reproduced from the questionnaire. Look them over and answer them now before you read on.

1. What do you consider to be your primary loving relationship?

* * * * * *

2. What three qualities do you believe to be most condu- cive to the continual development of love and growth in this relationship?

* * * * * *

3. What three qualities do you believe are most destruc- tive to a loving relationship?

* * * * * *

4. What do you consider to be your major secondary relationship (parent, spouse, child, etc.)?

* * * * * *

5. What three qualities are most conducive to helping these secondary relationships to last and grow?

*   *   *   *   *   *

6. What would be, for you, an ideal loving relationship?

*   *   *   *   *   *

7. What advice would you want to give, based upon your experience, to someone seriously entering into a primary loving relationship for the first time?

*   *   *   *   *   *   *

Over 600 completed questionnaires were returned offering a wide variety from which to draw some meaningful conclusions. Two-thirds of the respondents were women, most of whom were between the ages of 30 and 60. One hundred eight were under 30. Seventy-six were over 61 years of age.

The educational level of these individuals was extraordinarily high. This may be due to the fact that the questionnaire was sent to a rather select sample as mentioned earlier. Since all the respondents had previously written for further information regarding relating, they were already geared toward personal growth and understanding. All the respondents had at least a high school education. One hundred thirteen had completed a master's degree and 96 had some education beyond that.

It is obvious that the respondents in this study formed a rather unique segment of the population. I feel certain that if a less formally educated, less affluent group were questioned, the responses would be quite different. For example, in some similar sociological studies, especially among the poor in our society, such things as financial security, sexuality, and the basic day-to-day struggle for human survival were stated as paramount to relating. It would be most relevant for someone to replicate this study with a variety of different populations.

Of those responding, better than two-thirds of the individuals stated that their primary relationship was with a husband or wife. The remaining individuals saw family members, mother, father, sister, brother, or their children as their primary relationships.

The second largest group stated they were single, but primarily relating to someone of the opposite sex. A few had formed what they described as being meaningful homosexual relationships. A very small group stated their primary relationship was with themselves. Some mentioned animals such as pet dogs, cats, or birds. Only nine individuals said they presently had no primary relationship with anyone.

The vast majority had been in a single specific primary relationship from 11 to 25 years, with a large group, 90, having been together for over 25 years. Less than one-third of the respondents had been divorced and most of these were either actively involved in seeking a new, more lasting relationship, or were simply waiting for what they called a period of "recuperation."

When asked to share three qualities of primary relationships which they felt were most enhancing to continued growth in love, the population of this study responded that the most essential qualities were (in order):

> Communication
> Affection
> Compassion/Forgiveness
> Honesty
> Acceptance
> Dependability
> Sense of humor
> Romance (Including sex)
> Patience
> Freedom

It was interesting that communication, affection, forgiveness and honesty were mentioned as the top qualities by more than 85 percent of *all* the respondents! They defined communication as the desire to be open, to share, to relate, and to actively speak and listen to one another.

Affection was seen as the traits of caring, understanding, respect, physical and psychological closeness, nurturing, and kindness. Most of the respondents were clear to differentiate affection from sex and romance which, interestingly enough, was listed in the bottom three.

Compassion, the third most often listed, was defined

as the ability to have empathy, to forgive, to be supportive and selfless.

Honesty, which almost tied for third choice, was seen as the quality of being able to reveal true feelings at the moment, to verbalize fears, angers, regrets, and expectations.

This same group was also asked to identify those qualities or traits which were most destructive to a growing, loving relationship. The results were remarkably consistent. They reflected the opposite, negative aspects of the list of positive qualities.

Qualities destructive to a loving, growing relationship (in order):

Lack of communication
Selfishness/Unforgiving
Dishonesty
Jealousy
Lack of trust
Perfectionism
Lack of flexibility (not open to change)
Lack of understanding
Lack of respect
Apathy

It is interesting to note that both lists were topped by communication skills. It was again chosen by an overwhelming number (over 85%) as the quality which, when present, was conducive to loving and the most destructive when absent.

The lists were also internally consistent, with qualities such as honesty, affection, compassion, acceptance and dependability appearing as vital on both lists.

These results seem to indicate that the respondents had been careful about their responses, revealing a high degree of thought and interest.

Often when we talk about a relationship, we seem to limit our thinking to a most restricted group, that is, a man and a woman in a premarital (dating) or married state. We seem to ignore the myriad of other possible relationships in our lives equally dynamic and vital, such as, mother-father-son-daughter-cousins-uncles-aunts-grandparents-in-laws-coworkers, and so many others. We assume that these relationships are "different" and, therefore, require other skills and qualities than we need for successful primary relationships. To check this the questionnaire also asked that the respondents look at their secondary relationships and make the same classifications as to which qualities enhance these relationships and which destroy them. It was not surprising to find that the qualities necessary for growth in *any* relationship were the *same for all,* different only in *degree,* not *kind.*

Communication was again mentioned as the greatest enhancer of secondary relationships. Following this were: Honesty, Acceptance, Forgiveness, Concern/Consideration, Understanding, Affection, Respect, Sharing, and Sense of humor.

The respondents also selected those qualities which, when absent, were most conducive to destroying a secondary relationship. They were, in order of mention: Lack of communication, Dishonesty, Egocentric behavior/Lack of forgiving, Lack of time, Lack of trust, Jealousy, Apathy, Lack of affection, Lack of understanding, and Judgmental behavior.

It becomes apparent that the behaviors and qualities which enhance *all* loving relationships among human beings are the same. If we desire to come closer to our wives, husbands, lovers, children, coworkers, neighbors, or whomever, it will require the same skills, the same behaviors, the same qualities. It seems wise, therefore, for us to look at these qualities in some depth, for if we are desirous of loving each other, overcoming loneliness, and sharing our day-to-day lives in joy and peace, we must understand the dynamics of the qualities mentioned. The discussion of these qualities forms the basis and purpose of this book.

CHAPTER 1

A
Loving
Relationship

*Tenderness emerges from the fact that the two
persons, longing, as all individuals do, to
overcome the separateness and isolation to which
we are all heir because we are individuals, can
participate in a relationship that, for the moment,
is not of two isolated selves but a union.*

ROLLO MAY

"What happened," I asked her, "after having been together for so long? What happened?"

"I don't know," she answered. "I just don't know."

This dialogue seems inconceivable. We are all so much an active part of so many loving relationships, yet we have spent so little time considering the dynamics of what makes them work. Each day, for example, we interact with significant people who will affect our well-being, such as husbands, wives, parents, sons and daughters. We treat our encounters with them with care-free casualness. We seem unconcerned that they have any real influence at all. We ignore the fact that they have the power to bring us laughter or tears, joy or despair. These same relaxed attitudes are insidiously at work in our relationships with coworkers, neighbors and friends. We are certain that our relationships will naturally take care of themselves.

Most of us have never felt compelled to examine our relating and explore that what we feel, what we say, and what we do, affects it. It is imperative that this be done. Our relationships influence our mental health, our role in society and the family, our friends and lovers, and the groups to which we will belong.

Though I have valued the importance of loving relationships all my life, it has only been within the past 12 years that I have actively engaged in the study of relating. It doesn't seem like a great deal of time. Still, when I've reviewed the disappointing, almost nonexistent literature in the field or questioned others about the extent of the energies they have put to the task, even 12 years seems impressive.

My interest in loving relationships has led me to engage in both formal and informal studies. Whenever I have found someone such as myself actively seeking ways to relate with others in varying levels, I eagerly do my informal research. It makes for stimulating conversation. When I ask them if they feel happy and fulfilled in their present relationships, their answers intrigue and surprise. The most common replies given are, " I guess so." "Some of the time." "I haven't thought much about it." "I get along." "I have my highs and lows, what more can I expect?" Not very stimulating or inspiring. It is sad to find that very few answer an unequivocal, "Yes!"

I continue by asking if they have had any formal schooling in relationships, or have given any real serious thought to the subject over the years. Reactions to this have ranged from "Formal schooling in relating? Where do I get that?" "Well, I've thought about it some. I guess I'm as good at it as anyone else," to "Study relationships? You just form them and suffer the consequences."

I can't help but wonder if these individuals would ever consider voluntarily jumping in the sea without some knowledge of swimming, some water survival skills. I ponder why they are content to remain year after year in less than happy, unrewarding relationships when it could be otherwise. I speculate whether they suspect that relationships are capable of changing, growing and providing them with extraordinary dividends of love, warmth or security. I question if they are aware of the fact that a loving relationship can nourish as no other form of human interactive behavior, that positive, long-lasting, loving relationships give our lives the most fundamental meaning.

In order to elaborate on these questions in a more academic manner, I used the questionnaire previously discussed. I asked the recipients to define a loving relationship as they saw it. The responses were often excellent, sensitive and aware. Some of the respondents refused to attempt a definition at all. Many of the participants made statements as to the challenge and the educational value of being presented with such a question and took delight in answering it. For example one said, "You caused me to finally put into concrete terms what I had always taken for granted for so many unhappy years." Another commented, "I can't believe how difficult it was to put into words and thoughts, acts that I had lived through for 52 years."

It is interesting to note how easy and very human it is to put off such challenging concepts as love and relationships as being natural phenomena which will take care of themselves and which require no real serious thought. Before sharing the responses here, perhaps each of you will take time to define a loving relationship as you see it.

How do you define a loving relationship?

*   *   *   *   *   *

How the respondents defined a loving relationship?

● A loving relationship is a choice partnership. Loving someone in which even imperfection is seen as possibility and, therefore, a thing of beauty; where discovery, struggle and acceptance are the basis of continued growth and wonderment.

● A loving relationship is one in which individuals trust each other enough to become vulnerable, secure that the other person won't take advantage. It neither exploits nor takes the other for granted. It involves *much* communication, much sharing, and much tenderness.

● A loving relationship is one in which one can be open and honest with one another without the fear of being judged. It's being secure in the knowledge that you are each other's best friend and no matter what happens you will stand by one another.

• A loving relationship is one in which the individuals involved grow in their understanding and loving acceptance of each other's differences and encourages each person to reach out and share as much beauty and love as is possible to find.

• A loving relationship is one in which you accept the other person at the moment as a whole and receive that same acceptance.

• A loving relationship is one in which the distinctions of personal rights, possessions, thoughts, emotions and even actions become blurred, and it doesn't matter, because we share as much as is humanly possible with the same ultimate goals.

• A loving relationship is a mystical, yet concrete, dynamic experience, fluid, an end in itself rather than being a means to some end, where there are no expectations of the other, yet a deep appreciation of the relationship because of its intrinsic value, its possibilities, its wonder and its truth as it is experienced with the other.

• A loving relationship is one in which there is a mutual caring about the growth and progress of each, where possessiveness gives way to offering the other to be his/her own person, where selfishness gives way to selfless giving, sharing and caring, where the lines of communication are kept open, where the good in each is maximized, the bad minimized.

• A loving relationship is one in which each person

fearlessly allows a deep awareness, knowledge of the other, and sensitivity, to grow between them, with the understanding that no one is perfect, but that love is perfect, and therefore, as the basic tool for relating, can solve all problems.

• A loving relationship is the unconditional acceptance of another person. Helping him or her to attain personal goals, to grow and encouraging that growth. Each sees the other as a friend who can be trusted, depended upon and enjoyed.

• A loving relationship is one which offers comfort in the silent presence of another with whom you know, through words or body language, you share mutual trust, honesty, admiration, devotion, and that special thrill of happiness simply in being together.

• A loving relationship is one of trust and acceptance which creates a tender warm feeling of security and contentment. It offers unlimited support and strength upon which one can always draw.

• A loving relationship is an undemanding exchange of affection and concern, rooted in total honesty and continuing communication without exploitation.

• A loving relationship is *not* defined by length of time, but rather by quality of caring. At its best, it is a healthy, mutual exchange of thoughts, feelings and experience. It is *Home for one's soul* — a place to be ourselves and explore our deepest, inner yearnings, hopes, fears, and joys, without fear of condemnation, rejection, or being abandoned. It is an environment within which we can relax, are comforted, and gain the strength to fight the daily battle.

• A loving relationship is one in which the loved one is free to be himself — to laugh with me, but never at me; to cry with me, but never because of me; to love life, to love himself, to love being loved. Such a relationship is based upon freedom and can never grow in a jealous heart.

• A loving relationship is one in which both parties feel so loved, so accepted and so safe that they can share their innermost feelings, dreams, failures, successes, without reservation. It is a give-and-take, two-way reciprocal interaction rooted in mutual respect and cloaked with dignity, where tears and smiles are of equal importance and one that continually nurtures and supports growth.

• A loving relationship is like an ideal "home" — within it you can totally be yourself, be accepted, understood, trusted and respected as a valuable being. It is a nurturing environment where effort is made to provide enough caring and security so that one can share hopes and fears and where one is encouraged to learn and grow.

• A loving relationship is a wanting to celebrate, communicate, and know another's heart and soul.

• A loving relationship is being able to express feelings frankly and honestly with child-like spontaneous trust and openness.

• A loving relationship is one in which each one sees the beloved not as an extension of self but as a unique, forever becoming, beautiful individual — a situation in which the persons can bring their own special *I* to each other, a blending of selves without the fear of loss of self.

• A loving relationship is a reciprocal, active, changing bond that allows, encourages, in fact, almost demands using all the qualities necessary so that the lover will be all that he or she can be.

It's obvious and rather exciting that, as with all things, we define our own loving relationships. What is important is not so much what the definition includes, but that it is defined in our mind and agreed upon by the individuals forming the relationship. For some, a relationship will require total honesty, trust and commitment. For others a less restrictive involvement will be essential. It would be well to think about the constellation of possibilities suggested when we say "Come into my life. I love you."

CHAPTER 2

Loving Each Other Through Communication

We have developed communications systems to permit man on earth to talk with man on the moon. Yet mother often cannot talk with daughter, father to son, black to white, labor with management or democracy with communism.

HADLEY READ

Communication, the art of talking with each other, saying what we feel and mean, saying it clearly, listening to what the other says and making sure that we're hearing accurately, is by all indication the skill most essential for creating and maintaining loving relationships.

In his Nobel Prize speech in 1950, the great American author William Faulkner said,

> I believe that when the last ding-dong of doom has clanged and faded from the last worthless rock hanging tideless in the last red and dying evening, that even then there will still be one more sound: that of man's puny, inexhaustible, voice still talking.

There is little doubt that Mr. Faulkner was right. The world is full of talk. It seems that most of us are continually, often even in our sleep, engaged in some sort of communicative activity, mainly talking (even if it is to ourselves). We have joy talk, hate talk, fear talk, peace talk, pain talk, guilt talk, hope talk, threat talk, regret talk, esthetic talk, envy talk, spite talk, pure information talk and, among it all, hopefully some love talk. The hope lies, as Mr. Faulkner continued in his speech,

> . . . not simply because man alone among creatures has an inexhaustible voice, but because man has a soul, a spirit capable of compassion, sacrifice and endurance.

It is the compassion talk, the sacrifice talk, the commitment talk that though too seldom heard, remains the singularly most valuable stuff of which loving relationships are made.

Several years ago, when I was teaching my Love Class, we decided to attempt an assignment. We agreed to approach those people in our lives whom we valued and loved and express verbally that we "truly loved and appreciated them." We found that what appeared on the surface to be a simple, natural thing was rather more difficult than what we had imagined. Most of the students were lovingly tongue-tied. They felt ill at ease, awkward, even embarrassed by expressing their love. Several never completed the assignment. When we discussed and shared our experiences we agreed that it was strange indeed that so many found it threatening to communicate love! It then became obvious why we hear the voice of love so seldom and when it is heard it is spoken so softly, so shyly. This is true even though we have learned that unexpressed love is the greatest cause of our sorrow and regrets. We usually wait until people have died to express their value in our lives, to honor them publicly and to express our love for them.

As I have shared so many times before, I was fortunate to have been raised in a family where one heard a great deal of love talk. It was not always soft, sweet, and gentle, and what one expects to hear. Mama talked loudly. In fact, she often shouted. She had not read the psychological sage's advice, "Don't ever shout or strike your children. Verbal and physical wounds may scar forever." I heard verbal threats such as, "te spacco la faccia," which translates freely, "I'll smash your face!" Which, I must admit, she did on occasion. In fact, I have a broken front tooth to attest to the fact. Her favorite American expression (I've never understood why or where she picked it up), was, "Shut up!" Papa wasn't afraid that a good smack would permanently wound our psyches, either. He didn't know nor care a damn about psyches. He and Mama had values which they wanted us to share. Somehow, we never questioned that these were being taught for our "own good." But this peppery environment was never lacking in more gentle expressions of love as well. Mama never went to the Grand Central Market without bringing us all a bit of chocolate, or a favorite cookie or piece of fruit. Papa and Mama always hugged us "hello," "good night," and "good morning." They kissed us often, during the day and into the night. Wounds heal quickly when one knows unquestionably that love is there.

In love they shared God for our soul, schools and conversation for our minds, and delicious foods for our bodies. Mama also insisted upon a loving yearly physical "spring cleaning" — a fasting period accompanied by Citrate of Magnesia! Our reward was priority for the day in bathroom use (always crowded beyond belief being the only bathroom for our large family!) and the promise of our favorite meal the following day. No matter what our age we all were assured a vital role as a participant in the family. We were encouraged to talk about our joys, hurts, fears, disappointments and loves. When we had a problem it was a *family* problem to which we were all expected to offer verbal solutions. We were heard and what we said was respected. In this environment, life's lessons, rightly or wrongly deserved, were easy to tolerate.

One of the greatest complaints among the young today is that though they are given so much in terms of objects, money, and physical comforts, they feel deprived of close communication. They miss the type of talk which helps them to hear their own voices, discover their own resources, make their own mistakes and seek their own solutions in a supporting environment. They often feel that true communication between themselves and those they love is, if offered at all, of limited value.

A sensitive student of mine came to see me regarding a very personal problem. When I suggested that she discuss this with her parents she told me she never could, that they would never understand. I persuaded her to "give it a chance" because her problem would require family support. She returned several days later to report that she had sincerely tried but even when she confessed to her confusion and despondence, they minimized it and changed the subject, assuring her that she was "making a mountain of a molehill," that "she'd outgrow it," etc. They actually refused to discuss it, as if to ignore it would make it go away. It was only after a suicide attempt on her part that her parents reacted. "Why didn't you tell us you were having problems?" they asked! "Why didn't you listen when I did?" she said simply.

Eric Berne, the eminent author of *Transpersonal Psychology,* was concerned with bringing people together again in intimacy. He showed us how the many roles and games we played were breaking down communication, distancing us from each other and destroying any possibility of our becoming intimate with caring friends or lovers. He concerned himself with four questions — so vital in the communication process:

How do you say "hello"?

How do we say "hello" back?

What do we say after we say "hello"?

And, most of all, what is everybody doing instead of saying "hello"?

Good questions!

My concern will further complicate matters for I want to better understand the communication of *love*. My questions will add an element of complexity and daring, going beyond "hello." I'm concerned with:

How do you say "I love you" and why is it so very difficult to say such a positive statement?

How do you say "I love you" back without intimidation or fear?

What do we say after we've said "I love you"?

How do we keep the loving communication flowing?

And, most of all — what is everyone doing instead of saying "I love you"?

It is a known fact among those who study communication that most of the time we are talking to ourselves. Not only are we often not clear about what we want to communicate, but we lack the linguistic facility to put it into some sane semantic structure. Even when we do, the listener is often uninterested, unwilling or unable to "translate" the intellectual and emotional content of what is said. Communication becomes no more, then, than air in vibration.

The fine art of conversation, too, has all but disappeared. Cocktail parties and large dinner gatherings are conducive mostly to noisy, insignificant dialogue. Family dinners, which in the past offered us a time to share and talk have become little more than a ritual to be accomplished, leading to the dash for the television set, the evening's entertainment or the privacy of our separate rooms.

Lois Wyse, in her very special book of poems called *Lovetalk,* puts it most dramatically. She says —

> So many television marriages -
> that playing out of lives against a
> background of the tube.
> Instead of two lives filling the room,
> There are their two lives and the eleven o'clock news
> with
> Constant commercial interruption.
> Instead of what you say and what I say
> It is what Dick and Johnny and their guests say.
> You don't laugh with me;
> I don't laugh with you.
> All the wit comes pouring out of the tube.
> And we laugh at it together.
> The more we avoid talking

the more passive the relationship becomes.
Television permits us to walk through
life
with minor speaking parts.
And the more we fail to speak,
the more difficult speaking becomes.

How do you say "I love you"?

To a more or less degree all of us have language. Even though there are many theories, no one is certain about how it is learned. We do know that no infants are ever taught formally to talk, but unless they are severely neurologically damaged or mentally retarded, they will acquire language around the age of two. All the world's children develop language in the same way at the same age. They will babble, go through an initial stage called "echolalia," will proceed to words, then sentences. This, even though it is one of the most complex of human skills. All they seem to need is a language-filled environment where they can hear the sounds of the language. I will never forget an American lady whom I met while teaching in Taiwan, who stood back in awe and said, "Imagine, two-year-old children in the streets are speaking Chinese!" What did she expect they'd be speaking, Greek?

We know that infants are amazingly attuned to the sounds of language and will learn what they hear. Of all the words they encounter in their first few years, isn't it amazing that an infant can differentiate "milk," "me," "mama"? The words they will hear will be the words they will learn seemingly without reason. These will also

59

be the tools with which they will organize their environment and interact with it. These words will be the essential human connection. If they hear "yes" and "love" and "good" and other positive symbols, then these will be the tools with which they will relate. Our children say "no!" long before they learn "yes" and often "hate" before "love." Where did the child in preschool who shouts, "I'm having a nervous breakdown!" learn this? Certainly not instinctively.

So we either hear the language of love in our environment or we do not. Either we learn the verbal symbols necessary to relate with each other or we do not.

How Do You Say "I Love You Back"?

After we have acquired language to some degree, how do we keep it growing? How do we use it for informative giving, for nurturing dialogue?

Probably the most common use made of language is for the purpose of imparting information, to inform someone of something, to explain something. The teacher instructs the class clearly, "Always print your name in the upper right-hand corner of your assignments." Ask teachers how many times papers come back with names on the left-hand side, the middle of the page or not written on the page at all. How often have you asked for black coffee and had the waiter immediately ask, "With cream and sugar?" Having language, obviously, has nothing to do with communication. Communication requires dialogue. Most of us constantly find ourselves engaging in monologues. The great philosopher Martin Buber was very much concerned with human monologue/dialogue. He writes of *technical dialogue,* the type of communication in which we give information, requiring no feeling, and it is received and acted upon. He then moves on to *monologue disguised as dialogue,* in which one individual speaks to the total indifference of the other. He illustrates this with what he calls *lover's talk,* in which both parties alike often enjoy their own glorious souls and precious experience.

A most amusing example of this is the dialogue between Candide and Cunégonde, the lovers of Voltaire's philosophical work *Candide.* Leonard Bernstein set this wistful conversation to music in his great comic opera based upon the Voltaire classic.

Performed operatically as a duet, the pair of lovers together, yet individually, look to the future and voice their fondest hopes and visions.

Candide envisions a little farm for the pair one day replete with chickens, cows, and vegetables.

Cunégonde longs for the luxury of a yacht, the excitement of parties, a luxurious life, and the glamour of jewels.

Each continues on until finally the aria ends with Cunégonde dreaming aloud of traveling the world and enjoying the high life. Candide continues his reveling, dreaming contentedly of a more rustic life.

Returning from their individual dreams, the lovers look at each other, she exclaiming her love of married life; he in perfect harmony, and happy in the knowledge of the rarity of agreement between lovers.

You can imagine how long that relationship lasts!

Buber continues by defining *true dialogue.* He sees it

as one in which the speaker has the other person's individuality and special needs in mind. He states that in this
type of communication "one sees in the passing parade,
not a crowd or a mass, but a collection of individuals,
each of whom, without exception, can be seen as a
person." Buber wants the major goal of all true dialogue
to be the welfare of the loved ones, and the enhancement
of their fulfillment, and continued sustenance and
unending respect for their potential. It is another way of
saying that, "I want what I say to stimulate you, to bring
you peace, to help you to grow to your ultimate potential.
I want what I say to bring us totally together. You have
dignity and therefore my interaction with you must offer
you all that you deserve, the *total me* at the moment."
Wouldn't it be wonderful to have such communication
with those we love? How splendid, rewarding and nour-
ishing it would be.

What Do You Say After You've Said "I Love You?"

Once we've opened the avenues of communication,
how do we keep them open?

It is obvious that there is more to communication than
what meets the ear. There are many kinds of language,
that of words, that of silence, that of action and that of
listening.

Words are wonderful, but they are not *things*. Words
stand for things but they are not the things they stand for.
For example we can see a female walking across the
street and identify her with the word "lady" or
"woman." Lady or woman is a symbol for the person
but the person is more than the symbol — she may be a

mother, a business person, a daughter, a mother-in-law, a lonely person, a joyous individual, etc., ad infinitum.

Words are just phonetic symbols (sounds) put side by side into some agreed-upon order and given a meaning. The object "car" for instance, could have been called a "jup" or "liz" or whatever. It would still stand for the object "car" if we didn't know the difference.

Mark Twain has a hilarious short story about Eve's interfering with Adam's charge to name all things in the world. Adam has a terrible time being creative. Eve on the other hand, names everything by characteristics. He, for instance, calls his environment The Garden of Eden. Eve corrects him and points out that the setting is nothing like a garden, but far more like a park. She, therefore, insists upon calling it Niagara Falls Park. The point, of course, is that words are simply tools with which we can organize our environment. We can call anything whatever we choose.

We learn words as very young infants. We have few resources other than words as symbols with which to organize our worlds. The significant people in our environment teach us our usable vocabulary — dictionary definition of words, the intellectual content of the word. We think with the words we acquire from them and we become what we think. But it is even more complex than that. To each word we think we also attach an emotional content. This is how we *feel* about what the word represents. For example, let's take the word *mother.* We can easily define the term as a *female parent.* That's true. It is the intellectual content of the word but it is also a very shallow definition depending upon our unique experience with mothers. Our experiences with this word can conjure up feelings of elation — "It will be great fun seeing mother." "There is nothing like mother's lasagna!" Or the sound of the word *mother* can bring out negative feelings — "Oh no! She's a drag!" "If mother is coming with us, I'm staying home!" It is obvious, then, that the emotional content of a word is of equal, if not more, significance than the intellectual content.

Words continue to elicit responses of hate, fear, anxiety, and avoidance, responses we learned as children when we first encountered the word and have never bothered to redefine as adults.

There are those who hate "_____" with a passion. There are others who are quick to condemn races, religions, customs, beliefs, based solely upon their response to the symbol attached rather than their actual experience. They avoid, distrust, and even desire to destroy individuals who the symbols represent. Communication with people who have these strong emotional sets breaks down, in most cases, before it gets started.

What is your response when you hear the words Communist, Jews, Atheist, Cancer, Rapist, God, Love, Hope, Forgiveness, Rapture? Have you ever stopped long enough to analyze these words in your present state of maturity? Much has happened to most of us in terms of sensitivity, experience and education from when we acquired these words, perhaps decades ago. Have you ever tried defining words and rewriting your own personal adult dictionary?

There were many such labels which caused me pain as a child. Dago, Wop, Poor, Catholic, Retard, Skinny. We

64

have, most of us, known painful labels. Many of us are still judged, excluded or included, loved or hated, because of labels. Millions of Jews were murdered by the Nazis, not because they were people, simply because they were Jews. Even today such murders are occurring because of political or religious labels all over the world.

So it is essential to know, if we desire to communicate, that we must be careful about the words we use, for they may be using us! We can and must control our words. We can change our definitions and our feelings relating to them. It is only in this way that we become free to control our lives, for the words we use will, in a very real sense, determine our belief systems and our actions. Use them rather than be used and narrowed by them!

Though words are still the major source of communication, they are not the only source. In fact, St. Exupéry said, "Words can be a source of great misunderstandings." We also talk to each other in wordless messages. When I see people on the street I almost always say, "Good morning. How are you?" Many times they answer, almost fiercely, "Fine!" I cannot help but wonder, "Then why the hell don't you tell your face?"

We talk to each other with smiles, with handshakes, with hugs, with laughter, with eye contact, with touching, holding, enfolding, and a myriad of gestures. These, too, are languages. Some of which may "speak louder than words." You can tell a great deal about a person when he or she shakes your hand. A hug can send off so many messages. A glance can suggest a thousand words. Still, not too many of us respect the power of wordless messages. We do not even think about what they are telling others about us.

I was recently in a hospital with a most serious cardiac condition. I had many nurses taking care of me day and night. It soon became apparent which nurses were performing routine duties and which were actually engaged in helping patients to heal. How a thermometer was put in my mouth carried a special meaning. So did taking my pulse, giving a backrub, taking a moment to greet me warmly with a touch. Wellness comes from within but communicated warmth helps to bring it forth. I had a room full of flowers and plants. It was a joy to share them through the ward. I'd take them and use them as an opening to friendship. "For me?" the other patients would ask, and already one could see expressions of joy on their faces, eyes taking on new life. Someone cares. I made friends in almost every room. The doctors made medical rounds in the morning and Buscaglia made love rounds for the rest of the day. My own health increased amazingly fast — and I could perceive attitudinal changes in many of the others almost daily. One man who, on my first visit had said, "Who the hell cares? I may as well die!" was walking around the ward with me before I left. To "say" is wonderful but to "do" can have even greater power. I had a Buddhist teacher several years back who taught me that "to know, *and not to do,* is not yet to know!"

Unless you enjoy talking to yourself, it takes two for human communication. This usually means one to speak and the other to listen. But listeners are as rare as sensitive speakers. Most of us have forgotten the fine art of listening. If we listen at all, which is rare, we have the static of our own preconceived ideas working constantly until, when all is said and done, we hear not what the person is saying but what we are prepared to hear. We often find that people have answers to our queries and solutions to our problems prior to our stating them.

I recently discovered that the average speaker can utter 125 words per minute. The listener can process about 400 to 600 words per minute. True listening is determined by how we decide to use the intervals. Are we preparing our own dialogue? Are we planning tomorrow's menu? Are we fantasizing about what we could be doing or places we might prefer being rather than where we are? Are we observing and sensing the person's mannerisms, clothes, grammar, sexual quotient? All these things often seem to be occurring at once and it's only afterwards when arguments ensue that we see how much was missed.

The pitfalls to true listening are expressed in a thoughtful poem *Listen* by an anonymous writer.

> When I ask you to listen to me and you start giving advice,
> you have not done what I asked.
> When I ask you to listen to me and you begin to tell me why
> I shouldn't feel that way, you are trampling on my feelings.
> When I ask you to listen to me and you feel you have to do
> something to solve my problems, you have failed me, strange
> as that may seem.

Perhaps that's why prayer works for some people.
Because
God is mute and He doesn't offer advice or try to fix
things.
He just listens and trusts you to work it out for yourself.
So please, just listen and hear me. And if you want to talk,
wait a few minutes for your turn and I promise I'll listen
to you.

Sharing, so vital to loving communication, stops when you sense the other person is not listening or caring, and the sad part is that often we are not given a second chance.

A third, and most vital level of communication is also nonverbal. It is communication through action. You may remember that Eliza Doolittle's love message in the great Lerner and Lowe musical *My Fair Lady* was "Show me!" If you love me, she shouts, don't just talk about it — show me in action! Do loving things for each other. Be considerate. Put your feelings into action. Make that favorite food. Send the flowers. Remember the birthday or anniversary. Create your own love holidays to celebrate — don't just wait for Valentine's Day.

Now, the final question.

What is everyone doing instead of saying, "I love you"?

We are mainly distancing, destroying, intimidating, disappointing, degrading, devaluing and we don't know how to change this. A new language of love can remake our minds. In their important book, *The Human Connection,* Ashley Montagu and Floyd Matson state that love is the highest form of communication. They say:

> Human communication, 'as the saying goes, is a clash of symbols' it covers a multitude of signs. But it is more than media and messages, information and persuasion; it also meets a deeper need and serves a higher purpose. Whether clear or garbled, tumultuous or silent, deliberate or fatally inadvertent, communication is the ground of meeting and the foundation of community. It is, in short, the essential human connection.

So, if you want to make the human connection in a loving relationship you may want to review the following:

● *Tell* me often that you love me through your talk, your actions and your gestures. Don't assume that I know it. I may show signs of embarrassment and even deny that I need it — but don't believe it, do it anyway.

● Compliment me often for jobs well done and don't downgrade but reassure me when I fail. Don't take the many things I do for you for granted. Positive reinforcement and appreciation works toward making sure I repeat them.

● Let me know when you feel low or lonely or misunderstood. It will make me stronger to know I have the power to comfort you. Feelings, unverbalized, can be destructive. Remember, though I love you, I still can't always read your mind.

• Express joyous thoughts and feelings. They bring vitality to our relationship. It's wonderful to celebrate nonbirthdays, personal Valentine's days. Give gifts of love without reason and hear you verbalize your happiness.

• When you respond to me so I feel special, it will make up for all those who, during the day, have passed me up without seeing me.

• Don't invalidate my being by telling me that what I see or feel is insignificant or not real. If I see and feel it — for me — it's my experience and therefore important and real!

• Listen to me without judgment or preconception. Being heard, like being seen, is vital. If you truly see me and hear me as I am at the moment it is a continued affirmation of my being as we help each other to change.

• Touch me. Hold me. Hug me. My physical self is revitalized by loving nonverbal communication.

• Respect my silences. Alternatives for my problems, creativity, and my spiritual needs are most often realized in moments of quiet.

• Let others know you value me. Public affirmation of our love makes me feel special and proud. It is good to share the joy of our relationship with others.

I know you're probably thinking that the above ideas

are not really necessary between lovers. They occur spontaneously. Not so. It is these very aspects of communication that are the cornerstones of a healthy loving relationship. They also make up the most beautiful sounds in the world!

CHAPTER 3

Loving Each Other In Honesty

*Truth, the whole truth and
nothing but the truth.*

LEGAL OATH

*There is no such thing as an absolute truth —
that is absolutely true.*

ANONYMOUS

*And Pilate said, "What is truth?" (He
cunningly didn't wait for an answer.)*

It's said that in the 4th Century B.C., Diogenes went in search of an honest man. With a lamp in broad daylight, he traveled everywhere, so he would have the best possibility of finding him. He didn't.

Psychological, philosophical and religious literature is full of warnings that a healthy, lasting relationship must be based upon honesty and truth. It is vital for us to believe that at least those we love and who love us will be truthful and honest with us. How can we survive otherwise? Still, it would be interesting to find if anyone reading these pages could, with integrity, say that they know a completely honest person. We generally disguise our own anxiety about answering this question by indulging in such semantic gymnastics as, "What do you mean by honest?" "How honest?" "Under what circumstances?" "With whom?" "Honest about things that matter?" These questions suggest that most of us feel that there are many kinds and degrees of honesty.

However honesty is defined, the fact remains that dishonesty is one of the prime determinants of failed relationships. It has caused families to separate, lovers to physically harm one another or even kill each other in what are referred to as "crimes of passion," businesses to be dissolved, even governments to crumble, and nations to fight their bloodiest wars. In dealing with truth which might ultimately create even a minor crisis, it seems often more expeditious to tell a lie. "As long as it doesn't hurt anybody," we rationalize.

A Louis Harris poll, reported in 1969 in *Time* magazine, revealed that six out of ten individuals in the United States felt that lying was justified at times. One percent of those questioned felt that lying was permissible in any situation, at any time; 58 percent said sometimes; 38 percent said it was never permissible to tell a lie, and three percent dodged the issue *honestly* and said they were not sure. In reality, I don't believe that many of us have thought it through clearly enough to have an opinion. We speak of "nothing but the truth," and lie on our income tax forms. We agree that "honesty is the best policy," but we'd never dream of telling most people, if asked, what we truly think of them. This attitude is certainly not unique among those of us living in the United States. The ancient Greeks were actually schooled in lying and were taught techniques to keep from getting caught. Their great philosopher Socrates was, in essence, put to death for telling the truth because his judges believed that his *truth* would corrupt their youth.

Ancient Chinese societies advocated a blend of guiltless dishonesty. Rather than encouraging an uncompromising approach to a truth which might cause pain to others they suggested a type of truth "for kindness' sake." To this day we are still teaching these values. Examples of dishonesty are rampant in almost every sector of society, at every level of interaction. They are to be found in the most casual of relationships as well as in the most complex of international politics. If individuals are not actually engaged in lying, they are indulging in creative half-truths or dodging the issues altogether. Some philosophers and sociologists acknowledge that it is questionable if an individual or a society of any size could actually survive if dedicated to the whole truth. Marcel Eck stated that, "a society in which all truths were blindly exposed would be more like hell than a paradise." "Not to speak the truth," he continued, "is sometimes a duty." It is often rationalized that most people don't want to hear the truth, anyway.

Our courts require us to take the oath of justice, "the truth, the whole truth, and nothing but the truth." We then sit by and watch as brilliant lawyers present subtle "versions" of the truth conducive to the welfare of their clients in a particular situation. They are not lying, they say in defense, they are but rearranging and adjusting the facts.

Advertisers will blatantly tell us that their product is the very best. They will guarantee us instant relief or pleasure if we use it regularly. They promise to cure our colds, help us fall asleep, lose weight, and find romance, satisfying sex, and everlasting love. Even the most naive of us knows that these are lies, but we hear them so often and become so desensitized to them, that they no longer offend. Some of us even buy the products advertised in the hope that there will be some truth in them.

Journalists, who give strong lip service to their dedication to bringing us the truth, often lie to gain access to the truth. Political leaders expound esoteric platforms, promising impossible feats which they assure us they

77

will accomplish if elected. They will balance the budget, eradicate crime, end wars, do away with poverty, and put "a chicken in every pot." Some even assure us that they will revitalize the family and bring morality back to a decaying society. Even after more than a hundred years of being assured of the American dream of freedom, justice, and equality for all, we still have hope. We are not stupid, just conditioned over the years not to expect the whole truth. Even law enforcement officials some-times use deceitful methods in order to elicit the truth from a criminal. Physicians speak of protecting us from the truth. Teachers and counselors often feel they must cushion the truth. So much have we come to live with this that it has reached the point where we perceive and accept these behaviors as harmless, trivial, even normal. We speak of them as well-intentioned, and say, "How nice to see you," to people we would rather avoid. "We must get together sometime," we say to individuals we dislike. "What an attractive hairdo!" we exclaim when we wonder if the hair stylist has ever been trained. There are those who express gratitude over unwanted gifts, gush over babies they dislike, and feign delight over conversation that is boring them to death. We write positive letters of recommendation for individuals we are eager to get rid of and hope never to see again.

We engage in these untruths, we say, in order to protect others from pain, from harm or to spare the innocent. It is no wonder, then, that we no longer view dishonesty as a negative behavior but rather as a con-doned necessary social skill. We continue to encourage deceit. We therefore practice it with a clear conscience and teach the processes to our children as part of their growing to sophisticated maturity.

I have seen situations where children, not yet schooled in deception, have told grownups what they see as truth, and are straightaway sent to their rooms or the principal's office. Then, in these same situations, we teach, with a straight face, that honesty is the best policy. When children are punished and lose face for telling the truth, they learn quickly about the wisdom of "the white lie."

I remember a study I did in a kindergarten class with five- and six-year-olds. I asked them what they should do if they did something bad. Should they tell their mothers? Most said no. "Why not?" I asked, " 'Cause she'd hit me," was the usual answer. "Is it better to tell a lie and not get punished, or to always tell the truth?" They were incredulous that I would even ask such a question: "Are you crazy?" they said. "It's better to lie!"

Piaget, the eminent child psychologist, tells a story in his book, *The Moral Judgement of the Child,* pertaining to lying behavior. He gave children the following proposition: Two children break cups. Their mother asked them who did it. The first child said it wasn't he, and the mother believed him. The second child said it wasn't he, and his mother didn't believe him, and punished him severely. Piaget then asked, "Are both lies equally naughty?" The children answered without hesitation, "No." "Which, then, was the naughtiest?" the psychologist asked. The children answered, "The one that was punished."

How often have we heard, "It's OK, as long as you don't get caught." Still, every lie, great or small, conveys some information. It is not the lie, so much, as the information it carries and ramifications possible. Even the most insignificant lie will have an effect upon the listener's choices and have some lasting effect upon her or his belief system. So a lie, even a little white one, can be responsible for an unlimited number of possible effects upon behavior.

The ramifications of a lie do not end with its telling. If, like truth, a lie produced but one reaction, it wouldn't be cause for too much concern for we'd have only a single choice to make, "to believe or not to believe." But as long as lies are presented with degrees of whiteness or blackness, we have limitless possibilities for choice and we are usually left with feelings of confusion, fear, uncertainty, resentfulness, and suspicion.

We have a very human need to believe, to trust each other. I think we'd go mad if we felt there was no one we could trust. It is through trust that our value systems grow and change. With the security and reassurance arising from trust we become more open to risk.

There are many kinds of interpersonal deception, some more destructive and pathological than others. They start with what some call the "benevolent" lie. This is the type which is most common in social situations. There is the person who has waited for five hours for your promised 2 P.M. telephone call. They are furious. Still, when you finally call and say, "I'm sorry," they'll respond calmly, "Oh, it's OK." We've all been involved in such lying. We'd love to tell them what we feel but we dare not. "Do you like my new coat?" "Oh, yes," we say, actually hating it, "It's lovely! So right for you!" "How come you didn't come to my party?" Not "Because I hate your parties," but, "I wasn't feeling well." The self-protective (ego-protective) lie is one used to make things more comfortable for us. When confronted, we answer "I didn't say that," or "You didn't understand."

The manipulative lie we use to make things happen for our convenience. We manipulate the truth for our welfare.

The impersonal lie, lying on income tax and expense accounts, for example, we call padding and feel that everyone does it and anyway, it's so insignificant that we assure ourselves it hurts no one.

The status lie we use to build our own egos. We engage in one-upmanship games to impress others. If they have accomplished something, we've done one better.

These are but a few categories of lies. We also have the cover-up lie, the conspiratorial lie, and so many others. I'm sure all of us could add to the list.

Most individuals do not consider these lies of sufficient magnitude to even warrant the name of evil. In fact, in some cases we are convinced that they actually benefit us or others. As mentioned earlier, these untruths are often referred to in the literature as "benevolent lies," and they are seen as kind, considerate, warranted.

The secretary of the great religious leader, Martin Luther, is quoted in a letter to Max Lenz saying that such lies are not against God and that he felt that God would be understanding of them and accept them. This, even though Revelations (22:15) groups liars with fornicators, murderers and idolaters, and denies them entry into heaven.

By deceiving in any way (as previously mentioned,

deception is always a choice), we infer that we merit a very special status. We feel it perfectly permissible to lie for our own purposes, but are often indignant that others would consider lying to us. Our casual dishonesty may seem of little consequence to us, but we often fail to consider that others may feel the same as we do upon being deceived. In addition, there is always an element of risk involved in lying. One's lie may be discovered. The deceiver must, therefore, be forever cautious to keep a record of falsehoods and, as time passes, is often forced to explain and rationalize with more and more lies. It is said that liars must have excellent memories, for once caught, their credibility is forever in question.

Honesty can be a complicated affair. For example, who is to determine the triviality of a lie? Who is to be the judge as to the magnitude of an untruth? Is there really a lie that is psychologically healthy, that causes growth rather than hurts, and from which no one is adversely affected?

Most of us have known the pain that comes from deception, especially when we are deceived by those we love. Our personal security is based upon the assumption that the information given us by those we love will be honest. When that is shaken, or taken away it is not surprising that our lives can be temporarily (or even, for some, permanently) shattered. When our love is strong enough, we may be able to accept the situation, or rationalize that it was not done with evil intent or a desire to create pain. We may even cope and accept the untruth with human tolerance. We recognize the humanness of the person. We forgive.

Clark Mustakas in his book *Creative Living* says,

Being honest in a relationship is at times exceedingly difficult and painful. Yet the moment a person evades the truth, central fibers of the self pull away and the person initiates a process of deception — a way of manipulating the other person by preventing the person from discovering "real thoughts and real feelings."

There are many ways to deal with truth and deception. Since lying and honesty are simply choices, we can let it be known that we select truth and reward it when it occurs. Many of us have found that truth is the best policy. If we failed to be truthful, the consequences, over time, often proved to be far more destructive and painful than the conflict the lie was meant to evade.

Since relationships are created by the day-to-day process of sharing reality, we cannot risk having a relationship built upon lies, even benevolent ones. The chance of deception becomes always possible as the basis for all future interaction. Your real self, then, to some degree, becomes permanently violated and all future interrelatedness assumes the possibility of a series of lies. Security in relating vanishes.

The choice of truth, which might have been the pragmatic test of deeper future understanding, has been overlooked. In this way, doubts are created which will influence the continuance of love and trust. Faith is broken. Our belief system is threatened. Even, at best, if the lie is resolved, an impenetrable scar is created over future vulnerability.

Only the truth can help us feel secure. Only truth can bring us the necessary trust needed for long-lasting relationships. Only truth, painful though it may sometimes be, can create a safe environment of unity and growth.

Certainly, truth with a capital "T" is difficult. Still it is at the core of a loving relationship. Trust is impossible without it. Where there is no trust there can be no love.

So, to lie or not to lie? Dr. Roger Gould says in *Transformations:*

> The truth, as best as we know it, must be our goal, no matter where it leads us. Every self-deception causes erroneous judgments, and bad decisions follow, with unforeseen consequences to our lives. But more than that, every protective self-deception is a crevice in our psyche with a little demon lurking in it ready to become an episode of unexplained anxiety when life threatens.
>
> The self-deceptions which are designed to protect us from pain actually end up delivering more pain. We fortify our deceptions to protect them from the natural corrections of daily life. The larger the area of our mind we find it necessary to defend, the more our thinking processes will suffer, we will not allow our mind to roam freely because new information might contradict our self-deceptions. The larger the self-deceptions, the larger the section of the world we are excluded from.

On the other hand, in one of the most definitive works on lying, *The Right to Lie,* the authors, Robert Wolk and Arthur Henley remark:

> A successful marriage is the product of lies as well as love. Although the partners' emotions and attitudes may complement each other well, they are two separate people and their feelings cannot possibly coincide all the time. A policy of total honesty would make them blurt out truths that could be needlessly hurtful or perhaps just untimely. This could wreck the delicate balance of give-and-take so necessary between husband and wife. Constructive, competent and considerate lies

can have a mutually protective effect and prevent the partners from stepping on each other's toes. That is why good lying makes good marriage.

In another place these authors state, "The family that lies together stays together." They are, of course, not speaking of life-destructive untruths, but the day-to-day dishonesty that may protect the relationship from constant trauma. They add:

> The only lie worth telling is an untruth that might alter a situation for the better. It must be justifiable, technically proficient, and appropriate to the occasion. To arrive at a sound decision about a lie, a would-be liar should weigh the possible benefits against the possible risks, a process somewhat akin to playing "truth or consequences" by oneself.

The authors even offer a test to measure if the lie is being analyzed objectively enough.

I am reminded of a young wedded couple, very much in love. The wife was totally unskilled in cooking. She had acquired a recipe from her mother for a meat casserole which she cooked during the first weeks of her marriage. She asked her young husband if he liked it. He knew that she worked hard to make it and was afraid that he would offend her. He said, "Oh, yes! Very much!" He hated it. She, believing that he really liked it, began to cook it quite regularly. Since she had difficulty breaking down the recipe, there were always great quantities of leftovers which had to be eaten. That meant that the casserole appeared many times during the week. Finally he could bear it no longer, and in a moment of anger, he confessed that he hated her cooking, that it gagged him, and he never wanted to see that casserole on his table again! She was shocked and hurt. He had *lied* to her. In tears she said, "I'll never believe you again!" Such a small thing. But an insidious seed was planted.

The tragedy is that often even such seemingly insignificant experiences mushroom, escalate, and finally create complicated and tangled webs of distrust that capture and destroy. If this is true, and statistics seem to substantiate this, then we may want to seek alternatives to deception. There seems to be no real reason why truth must hurt. Perhaps it can, if handled correctly, clear the air and offer a platform for change.

So, what to do? Deceive or not deceive? Since we are only humans, perhaps it is not such a cut-and-dried decision. But the problem should not be ignored, since it is responsible for such a large majority of unsuccessful relationships. Certainly, one can choose to deceive, but there may be alternatives to deception which might merit our consideration. In order to do this we must put aside the idea that deception may be good, that too often the truth hurts. We must be willing to face the fact that these beliefs may be no more than a comfortable "cop-out," that although truth may hurt, lying to one you love may do more than hurt, it may be almost totally devastating.

Truth in a relationship should begin at the start. Wise individuals, dedicated to growing together in mutual love and trust, whether lovers or possible business partners, should discuss their attitude and expectations regarding honesty early on in the relationship. Among other things, they must consider whether they tolerate lying. There will be some who would rather be lied to than have to face the truth. "To speak the truth among people who do not want to hear it," Nicholas Humphrey said once, "is considered almost an aggressive act — an invasion of privacy, a trespass into someone else's space. Not nice, not done." They may feel it is better not to know than to have to face the anxiety and pain that truth might bring. There are others who will want nothing but the truth, but will want the truth to be offered lovingly. Too often we equate truth with the "brutal reality." Not so. Truth can be communicated gently. "I'm not as fond of this outfit as I am of your blue one. But remember, it's only *my* opinion, and I'm not Yves St. Laurent." This is easier to take than "It's awful! I hate it!" If we decide to accept only the whole truth, then perhaps it can be communicated less harshly in statements like, "Remember, we decided to always be truthful with each other. So this is how *I* see it, or feel, *now.*"

It is realistic to believe that we shall have to deal with the conflict of honesty and deception for our entire relating lifetime. How can we expect total honesty with others when many of us engage in lying to ourselves? We must be willing to accept the fact that we may fall from truth from time to time. We must learn to accept these lapses as human and use them as learning experiences to reinforce more truthful behavior at a future time. But it seems to me that if we want our relationships to last and to grow, honesty and truth must be our inevitable goal.

CHAPTER 4

Loving Each Other In Forgiveness

Since nothing we intend is ever faultless, and nothing we attempt ever without error, and nothing we achieve without some measure of finitude and fallibility we call humanness, we are saved by forgiveness.

DAVID AUGSBURGER

Peter came to Jesus and asked, "Lord, how many times should I forgive my brother when he sins against me? Up to seven times?" Jesus answered, "I tell you not seven times but seventy times seven."

MATTHEW 18:21-22

Forgive. There is a wonderful aura surrounding the verb forgive, great warmth and strength. It is a word suggesting a letting go, a releasing, an action which has the power to soothe, heal, reunite and recreate.

I have a friend whose husband had been killed in an automobile accident. The "killer" was a middle-aged businessman, a husband and father of three. He was returning from a business lunch, drunk. He was found guilty of manslaughter, given the maximum sentence and sent to prison. "Forgive him?" my friend said incredulously. "I'd see him in Hell first. He's killed *my* husband and *my* children's father! He should be kept in jail forever." I wonder if she has any idea of how he has already suffered and must feel about the accident.

A woman who had been the victim of a mugger felt the same way. "He still haunts my life," she whispered, fresh tears of anger welling in her eyes. "He harmed me. He made me feel frightened and suspicious in a way that nothing can change. I hate him! And it doesn't make me feel any better to know he's in jail. What good is that? He deserves to die! I may get over my fears some day. But I'll never forgive!"

"I can't forgive my parents for screwing up my mind with their neurotic ideas. It's their fault that I'm afraid to live. Now that they're older they come to me for love. They can't understand why I avoid them. Now it's their turn to suffer!" a student of mine told me.

"Since our divorce my wife tries everything to keep me away from my son. Sure, I made a stupid mistake. I hurt her. But she's taking out her revenge in a terrible way. I've told her I'm sorry and I am. What else can I do? I can't erase what I've done. I'm not any less of a person now than the man she loved and married. It's just not in her to forgive."

A victim of the Holocaust argued that to forgive his torturers and the murderers of his family and friends was tantamount to condoning their brutality. "As long as I live I'll hate them and pray for their apprehension and retribution, justice still lives in me. Imprisonment, or even their death, will never make up for all they did, but it will, at least, show that there is some right left in the world."

These are all very real and painful situations. Being wronged, physically or psychologically abused, creates deep wounds. It seems simply human and natural to demand justice, to desire "sweet revenge."

Forgiving others, as difficult as that may be, is only a part of the problem. It is often just as difficult to forgive ourselves for what we perceive as our having wronged. A vivid and popularly known example of this can be found in William Styron's excellent novel, *Sophie's Choice*.

Sophie, a victim of Nazi madness and sadism, is forced to make a choice. She must decide which of her children is to die and which is to live. She is asked to make this decision at once, the alternative being that if she does not, both children will be killed. She makes the horrible choice. Though her life continues, she is overwhelmed with feelings of guilt. Her expiation comes only after she forms a self-destructive relationship with a mentally sick man who finally kills and frees her.

A minister told me of a man who calls him almost weekly with terrible feelings of guilt. He decries the fact that he never gave his wife the trip to Honolulu she so often dreamed of prior to her death. He accuses himself, even after years, of having hurt her and kept her from the happiness she so justly deserved.

On the other hand, I recently heard of a woman in Florida who was raped, shot in the head, brutally mutilated and left to die. Astoundingly, she survived the ordeal. Her head wound left her permanently blinded. In a television interview the host was reflecting on the bitterness she must feel, the unhealing scars she would have to deal with for the remainder of her life. Her astonishing reply was something to the effect of, "Oh, no! That man took one night of my life, I refuse to give him one additional second!"

The New York Times carried a story which caught the eye of many. It concerned a husband and wife who had gone to prison to embrace, in forgiveness, the man who had raped and murdered their 22-year-old daughter. Bob and Goldie Bristol's story is sensitively recounted in a book called *When It's Hard to Forgive*. In the book they tell of the horror and pain they felt in learning of their daughter's murder and their eventual decision to leave retribution to heaven. Fortified with a deep sense of religiosity, they decided to embrace their enemy in love. After many attempts to reach Tom (the fictitious name they assigned to their daughter's slayer) he finally agreed to see them. Mrs. Bristol describes their meeting in prison with touchingly simple language:

> The door opened; Tom entered the room. He was about 6 feet tall, dark-haired and muscular, cleanly dressed and shaven. . . . a person. God's love welled up within me and overflowed. Tom paused, his eyes filling with tears. My husband and I stood and each in turn embraced Tom. We wept together.

She frankly admits that they did not understand the "why" of his brutal actions. They simply allowed themselves to experience his humanness, the aspect of Tom they were able to identify with, understand and accept.

After their meeting, they felt free, purged of anger and resentment. Even their pain disappeared. For unexplained reasons, Tom felt otherwise and refused to continue the relationship and accept their forgiveness. He broke off contact.

Afterward, Mrs. Bristol was often invited to speak at public meetings. People were intrigued with her experience and the dynamics of forgiveness. She was surprised to find that so many of her audiences were hostile toward her. She was frequently attacked as unfeeling and accused of betraying her daughter's worth and memory. She was seen as unloving and accused of having a naive, detrimental approach to social and societal ills.

It is commonly accepted that every religion has, at its heart, deep commitments to compassion and forgiveness. It is obvious that though it may be simple for the gods to forgive, it is difficult, indeed, for human beings.

Asking for forgiveness and forgiving others is a complicated process that involves our deepest empathy, humanity and wisdom. Historically we have found that without forgiveness there can be no lasting love; no change, no growth, no real freedom. In *Love is Letting Go of Fear,* Dr. Gerald Jampolsky states:

> Hate, bitterness and vindictiveness are overpowering, self-defeating and intellectually as well as emotionally depleting.

It is important, then, for those who care about lasting relationships to better understand the dynamics of forgiveness. Certainly, if we are to live together as the frail and vulnerable individuals we are, we will have great need of it.

Forgiveness is an act of will. It is a volitional choice. We either choose to forgive or we do not. But we must remember that to be forgiven and to forgive involve the same dynamics. If we hope to be forgiven for wrongdoing, then we are compelled to do the same. If we are unable to forgive others, we cannot expect others to forgive us.

When we give ourselves in love we become our most vulnerable. We are never safe. We become open to disappointment and hurt. In a relationship, individuals come together with separate histories and experiences. They do this in the hope of creating new worlds by writing and living out and sharing new experiences together. But this is not easy, since we all interact in the shadow of past fears, expectations and habits, since we are all different, all imperfect, it is seldom possible without encountering conflict.

When we feel wronged, we immediately look to the other for blame. We perceive ourselves as victims. Something has been done to us, "the innocent." We have a right, therefore, to demand justice. We believe that justice has been accomplished only when we can hurt those who have hurt us, disappoint those who have disillusioned us, make suffer those who have injured us and given us pain. They must experience our revenge at once and preferably continue to experience it forever. We are certain that wrong will be righted only in this way. Only then will the slate be wiped clean and our pain disappear. After all, we rationalize, it was the other's fault. (Aren't we always sure that it was the other's fault?) Why then should we be the one to suffer? We seek vengeance for we know that the experience will be sweet. But do we find it so? How many of us have gone to great pains to avenge a wrongdoing, only to find that once we have had our revenge we have accomplished little more than finding ourselves loveless and alone? What satisfaction is there in causing another to suffer if our pain still remains? What is the use of demanding an eye for an eye — when having plucked out the other's eye, we still have only one eye?

When wronged by those we love, we seem to devalue years of relationship — a relationship that may have brought us many joys and which required much intellectual and emotional energy to have lasted so long. Still, with a single harsh statement, a thoughtless act, an unfeeling criticism, we are capable of destroying even the closest of our relationships. We quickly forget the good and set out to rationalize scenarios of hate. We do this rather than take up the challenge of honest evaluation and confrontation. We ignore the possibility that in the act of forgiving and showing compassion we are very likely to discover new depths in ourselves and new possibilities for relating in the future. We are too proud. We engage rather in self-defeating activities which keep us from forgiving; beliefs that if we withdraw and run from the situation we will hurt the other and absence will heal us; the fantasy that in avoidance there can be closure; the naive hope that in hurting, shaming, blaming and condemning we will be made to feel better. We fail to realize that when we refuse to engage in forgiving behaviors, it is we who assume the useless weight of hate, pain and vengeance which is neverending, and, instead, weighs upon us rather than the wrongdoer.

Of course, forgiving is not an easy process. Our rational mind is not sufficient to instantaneously break through the intricate web of feelings which overcome us when we are wronged. It seems more simple to look for ways to escape our pain. Rather than deal with it, we blame, we accuse, we condemn, we exclude, we damn. Forgiveness can never be realized in an atmosphere of accusation, condemnation, anger and fault finding.

We will only begin to forgive when we can look upon the wrongdoers as ourselves, neither better nor worse. We need to remember that we coexist as mortals in the world, together, the wronged and wrongdoer, and that, in our common humanity, the situation could readily be reversed. It is difficult for us to imagine that, but for circumstances, we might have been a part of the fanatical Hitler youth or the sick and frightened sociopath who cannot evaluate appropriate behavior. It is often impossible for us to accept the fact that "there but for you go I." Yet this is so. We divide the world into the good and the bad and see ourselves as being on the good side, distancing us from the other. Yet, it is only in identifying with the other that the processes of understanding and forgiveness can begin.

Individuals are incensed when it is suggested that they could, under certain situations and circumstances, be a part of any behavior harmful toward their fellow human beings. Yet, innocently, they do so every day. They ignore antipollution laws, refuse to accept responsibility for inferior education, world hunger, the loneliness of their neighbors, the ill-treatment of children and the elderly. They are only too ready to condemn the politicians, the activists, the Communists or anyone else rather than accept their own thoughtlessness. They are too caught up in the self to evaluate their own prejudicial, hurtful, negative attitudes. If we are perceptive we will find that either by choice or unconsciously each of us engage, almost daily, in some wrongdoing. But this does not mean that we are evil, that we lose our worth as loving human beings. One act is not sufficient reason to devalue a person.

There are good people who see their political, social or religious beliefs as right and sound, and who, therefore, feel free to engage in self-righteous wars which kill thousands of innocent individuals. They rationalize this by seeing these individuals as enemies who threaten their security and beliefs. The My Lai massacre is a case in point. It is too simplistic to condemn all those who participated in this disgrace as evil or worthless human beings. It is more difficult to try to evaluate the circumstances that could result in causing good people to behave in evil ways. We will only understand and forgive when we perceive these individuals with compassion — as feeling and vulnerable beings like ourselves, capable of weakness, confused idealism, fear, panic, cowardice, frailty. Sympathetic understanding, heart and mind felt identification with others are the necessary first steps in piercing the otherwise impenetrable walls of unforgiving attitudes.

This knowledge is repeated naturally, over and over again, in healthy, loving relationships. Parents often spend their lives overlooking their children's thoughtlessness. Children overlook their parents' possessiveness. Lovers squint at each other's faults and frailties. We do these things because we love these individuals and we know that we are not perfect either, because we see our long-range relationships as greater and more valuable than the momentary discomfort which an isolated negative act or attitude may inflict upon us. We continue to love those who hurt us from time to time, because we know that they are worthwhile human beings, capable of good as well as evil. We view them as human, open to the possibilities of change. In seeing them as such, our love is understanding and conducive to growth.

Love is the single greatest source of forgiveness. In love we are able to view the wrongdoer again as a worthy person. In love we put the wrong in perspective and view the act apart from the person. We do not overreact. We strive, through empathetic behavior, to erase the boundaries between wrongdoer and wronged, even when we do not understand the behavior. Through this process we come together, renew our faith, better understand and strengthen our present and move forward in trust again. "Forgiveness, then," says Dr. Jampolsky, "becomes the means for correcting our misconceptions; it allows us to see only the love in others and ourselves, and nothing else." This is the second step on the path to compassion and forgiveness.

This may sound more simple than it is. Though before we devalue the process, we should perhaps view the alternatives.

It might be interesting to consider why we choose to cling to a hollow revenge that can serve us no purpose, except to feed upon our creativity and keep us from loving. After all, the wrong is done. It is past and cannot be changed. We have only the present and future upon which to move forward.

A student of mine who had been cruelly jilted by her lover, said wisely, "I can't kid myself. I know I still love him or I wouldn't care what he did. And if I still love, I don't understand my intense need to cause him pain, to hurt him. These are crazy, conflicting feelings. I know what's rational in my head but my heart is irrational. It hurts! I know I've got to forgive, forget and go on living. He's gone and having a great time. I'm the one in pain, so I'm the one who's got to do something about it!"

The student recognized her pain. She knew she would have to somehow take full responsibility for her future.

To go on she would have to forgive the man she loved for her own sake, even though he hurt her. She knew that she did not *own* him. She valued herself enough to know she didn't want him if he did not want to be with her. She also knew that loving him should mean that she wanted him to be happy. If his being happy meant being free of her, then she could only step aside. This did not mean that she denied her disappointment, her anger, her intense feelings of rejection and loss. In fact, she felt her pain so intensely that for weeks she was unable to study or concentrate. She even contemplated dropping all of her classes. She tried but failed to build new relationships. She finally accepted the fact that if she wanted release from this painful quandary, she herself had to do it.

Emotional pain and psychological pain are at least as debilitating as physical pain. Few of us will escape these pains in our lifetime. It cannot be avoided. It can only be dealt with. Forgiveness is often the major, if only, out. As David Augsburger puts it,

> Forgiveness is letting what was, be gone; What will be, come; What is now, be.

It is a freeing of self from the past and facing the future wiser, with renewed hope and faith. Forgiveness is often called an unconditional gift of love. This implies, not that, "I will forgive you *if* or *when*," but, "I will forgive you because I must, if I ever hope to continue to live fully."

It was interesting that after my student finally and fully let go, her boyfriend returned, repentant and contrite.

She, by this time, felt no anger, no spite, no hate. She accepted him back prepared to continue their relationship with greater wisdom and at a new, more sensitive level. She felt that something had been lost but that what had been gained was of far greater value. She learned that she had not been alone in her suffering, he had suffered too. They were ready to build upon new possibilities based, not on their past mistakes, but their future alternatives.

Forgiveness is not always as wise and reasonable as this. Too often it is offered as a gift, the implication being the superiority of the giver. When so offered, it is not forgiveness. It becomes a bargain which brings with it loss of dignity, endless guilt and humiliation. It is a form of emotional blackmail with one party becoming the *generous benefactor* to the *inferior sinner*.

This nonforgiveness is, again, beautifully encapsulated by David Augsburger. He calls it "One-up-forgiveness" and describes it as implying,

> I have examined, weighed, judged you and your behavior and found you sorely lacking in qualities that are worthy of my respect. I have these qualities at this point in time, but you do not. I humbly recognize my superior moral strength and your weakness, my consistent moral behavior and your inconsistency of immorality. I forgive you your trespasses. We will henceforth have a relationship based on the recognition of my benevolence in the hour of your neediness, my generosity in the face of your guilt. You will find some suitable way to be dutifully grateful from this day forward.

This is not forgiveness! This is no more than a manipulative put-down. True forgiveness will become easier when we learn to empathize and apologize; when we admit we are human too, capable of wrongdoing; when we make allowances for circumstances we may not understand; when we have faith in the basic good of personkind, when we are willing to start again with compassion and without grudges. The Jewish word for compassion is derived from *rechem,* meaning *womb.* The inference is a new birth, suggesting a fresh start. This fresh start brings with it a deeper understanding of the futility of grudges, expectations, and unresolved hate and anger and renews our hope in the power of love.

There is another aspect of forgiveness even more demanding. It is a higher process built from forgiveness but surpassing it — forgetting. As long as we forgive, but maintain the memory of the hurt, the resentment, the feelings of being violated, as long as we live in the shadow of hurt, true forgiveness has not occurred. I have heard it said that to forgive and not forget is like "burying the hatchet in the ground with the handle sticking out." We are simply holding in a waiting pattern, ready for the next battle.

We fear forgetting for we believe this implies the washing of the wrong from the slate, condoning the wrongdoing, and accepting the responsibility for the other's evil action. We resent our having to forgive without some act of repentance or punishment on the part of the wrongdoer. But forgetting does not imply that we condone the wrong. It suggests that the action is past and for the future's sake it must be released so we can resume living again.

Too often, the process of recalling the past, in order to

better deal with the present and future, is a waste of time and serves little purpose. It becomes nothing more than a turning over and reliving of wrongdoings. This seems to serve mostly to enhance our discomfort, put us on our guard, enforce our anger and resentment and arouse our suspicions. Unless we are able to forget the past, we'll never be free of its power to reawaken hate and pain. We will be forever engaging in a nonproductive, endless process. It is well known that love does not keep a record of wrongs. Our need is to learn from wrongs, then, having become wiser, let them go and move forward into tomorrow.

Let's keep in mind that there is nothing wrong with us if forgiveness comes hard. We are simply human, vulnerable and far from perfect. The wrong the people do us is difficult to deal with, especially when we are innocent and can find no explanation for another's behavior. Why should we forgive and forget? We forgive, for the price we pay for not forgiving is too great. To bear grudges, to harbor hate, to seek revenge, are all *self-defeating* and lead us nowhere. They neither satisfy nor heal. They keep us from moving forward and starting again. They bury positive energies in negative actions which serve only to exhaust and deplete us. They keep us suspicious and hesitant to trust again. They destroy our creativity, and retard our growth.

There is no more personally rewarding moment than when we can truly forgive and are forgiven. At that instant we become really free, free to move forward as fully functioning human beings. Illusions of perfection, ours and the others, are shattered and we accept and are accepted as the vulnerable, imperfect human beings that we are.

Our greatest philosophers and religious leaders have also been our most forgiving persons. Through the Buddha's forgiveness and compassion, millions have been helped to insight and acceptance. Jesus of Nazareth was the model of forgiveness. He forgave the prostitutes, evil-doers, betrayal by his own disciples and, ultimately, even those who put him to death. They forgave even if it seemed against logic, against psychic reality, against what is often called "human nature." True forgiveness is an act of the highest of human behaviors. As a Buddhist teacher of mine once said, "Let go. Why do you cling to pain? There is nothing you can do about the wrongs of yesterday. It is not yours to judge. Why hold on to the very thing which keeps you from hope and love?"

As suggested in almost every holy book — *Judge not.* Try to understand and have empathy strengthened with compassion; then, forgiving is easy. It is the forgiver who is freed in forgiving. Leave judgment and revenge to heaven.

"Forgive us our trespasses as we forgive those who trespass against us."

CHAPTER 5

Loving Each Other In Joy

The only thing worth having in an earthly existence is a sense of humor.

LINCOLN STEFFENS

Happiness is a man's greatest achievement; it is the response of his total personality to a productive orientation toward himself and the world outside.

ERIC FROMM

No man is happy unless he believes he is.

PUBLIBIUS SYRUS, 50 BC

It seems to me that deep relating without joy, laughter, and a sense of humor is an impossibility. That is, perhaps, why all saints are said to be "transcendental clowns." Conrad Hyers, in his book, *Zen and the Comic Spirit,* suggests that "the demons of desire and attachment, ego and ignorance, may be exorcised through laughter, and point us to a kind of cosmic laughter that is to be entered on the other side of this exorcism."

I'm certain that we have all been reminded many times that life is not to be taken casually, that "it's damn serious business!" To a certain degree, this may be true. But, that seems to me to be all the more reason to maintain and develop a keen sense of humor. In fact, I know that I have been saved, again and again by my ability to see the humorous side of a situation, especially to laugh at myself and my imperfections. I know it takes courage, and a degree of borderline insanity, to smile and laugh in a world where, since the beginning of recorded history, we have continued to kill, rape, desert, and hurt each other. We've been, until now, unable to find reason for all of this. Perhaps the giving up of reason and the acceptance of our humanness as the ultimate joke may offer us another alternative.

Mother Theresa of Calcutta, who serves constantly

among the despairing, the hungry and the dying, requires that her hospital wards be filled with laughter. She sees the sound of laughter as the strongest force toward health, productivity, strength and spirituality. St. Francis of Assisi wandered the streets like a clown, laughing at despair. St. Theresa of Avila always looked for novices who knew how to laugh, eat and sleep. She was sure that if they ate heartily they were healthy, if they slept well they were more than likely free of serious sin, and if they laughed, they had the necessary disposition to survive a difficult life.

The symbol of the laughing Buddha, fat and healthy, represents the essential joy of Buddhism. In fact, among the Zen Buddhists, laughter and happiness are the core of their teachings. There is a level of humor to be found sprinkled lightly over every religious sect.

Philosophers throughout our history have stressed the necessity of joy for survival. In 451 B.C. Sophocles, for instance, reminded his students that, "The man from whom the joys of life have departed is living no more, but should be counted as dead." The philosopher George Santayana has said, "Happiness is the only sanction of life. Where happiness fails, existence remains a mad and lamentable experiment." "There is no duty we so much underrate," Robert Louis Stevenson reminded us, "as the duty of being happy." Even the constitution of the United States guarantees us "the pursuit of happiness" as part of our constitutional rights.

Still, in our time, there is pitifully little joy demonstrated. There seems to be something not quite right about those who are happy. It is common belief that there must be something wrong with contented people. We look at them as either fools, frivolous, or totally lacking in ordinary common sense. They are suspect.

Most of us actually feel guilty when we're happy! We're convinced that we will either be punished for it or that gloom will not be too far behind. D. Raymond Moody, in his fine book, *Laugh After Laugh,* states that,

> It is well to recognize that some persons are actually fearful of joy, elation, pleasure or other usually positive emotional states. In many of these people being joyful causes them to have feelings of guilt, shame or unworthiness.

This is certainly strange.

Scientists almost totally avoid the study of joy, laughter, humor and happiness and its relationship to human well-being. Lin Yutang writes, "I have always been impressed by the fact that the most studiously avoided subject in Western philosophy is that of Happiness."

It is rare that we hear spontaneous, uproarious laughter. If we do, we are certain that the revelers must be ne'er-do-wells or drunk. We pay large amounts of money to get professional comics to make us laugh. We tumble over with laughter when they mimic our "sane" behaviors and in this way reveal our follies. We love clowns. In strange attire, they participate in outrageous antics and engage in divine madness to help us see the simple truth about humanity. For a time, their behaviors set us free from the straightjacket of convention, the predictability of a routine life and expectations of behavior. They touch the deep desire within all of us to let go of inhibition and get in touch with our natural spontaneity, our natural madness. In a very real sense, we are all of us clowns — some more fearful and inhibited than others — but, nonetheless, potential clowns.

Comics view life through a microscope and are, therefore, able to show us clearly what we already know unconsciously, that life is a wonderful joke, and that we human beings, in our studied seriousness, are often at the center of it!

I was recently asked to help plan, with some friends, a "real Italian wedding." As with most ethnic groups, weddings are for Italians only slightly less important than births. In this case, the planning had taken on monumental proportions, all leading to loud, lusty arguments and empty solutions. It all reached a peak when it was announced that the mother of the bride was a vegetarian! What to do now with the mostaccioli and meat sauce! It took Grandma to set everything straight. Laughing all the time, she pointed out how silly everyone was being. "So, don't worry about the vegetarian. I'll stuff her a zucchini!" Everyone roared. The wedding was planned, and Giacomo Leopardi, the Italian philosopher, was proved right again when he said, "He who has the courage to laugh is almost as much a master of the world as he who is ready to die." We are funny! All we need to do to affirm this is to look about us. A wedding which should be the height of togetherness, love, and joy had almost come apart because someone didn't eat meat!

Observe people in airports, in crowds, at parties, on busy freeways. How can we keep from laughing? A man is just informed that his flight has been cancelled due to serious mechanical difficulties. He insists that the plane *must* fly or he will miss his Chicago connection! A lovely girl sits at a party, unwilling to make the slightest effort to mix, and leaves exclaiming what a dull party it was and how unfriendly the people were. A person pushes or shoves his way to the box office only to have to wait an hour for the movie to start. The driver goes at breakneck speeds to pass you up, only to have to wait at the next stop signal as you drive up smiling next to him. These are certainly laughable behaviors which we observe daily in our lives. Human beings are very comical creatures and life provides us with so many opportunities for laughter. Now, all we need is to learn to laugh again.

I remember an old Jacque Tati film called, "Mr. Hulot's Holiday," which began at a train station in which there was a mob of people waiting for a train to arrive at Track A. Suddenly there is a totally unintelligible announcement which comes through the speaker that produces a mad, inexplicable dash for Track B. After a moment there is another garbled announcement and the same crowd pushes its anxious way to Track C. At that moment the train arrives at Track A! I laughed about this for several minutes after the film was well into another episode for I relived the many times Buscaglia ran up and down platforms, a part of the crazy crowd! Situations such as these, I'm certain, have caused George Santayana to say, "Laughter, as I have come to see it in my old age, is the innocent youthful side of repentance, of disillusionment, of misunderstanding." Victor Borge said that, "Laughter is the closest distance between two people." There is no more sure way of coming together with other human beings than through laughter. George

113

Bernard Shaw, the great cynic/philosopher, agreed that only "by laughter can you destroy evil without malice, and affirm good fellowship without mawkishness." We have all known experiences when a shared laugh has changed what was just moments before a strained, anxious relationship into a warm, joyous, productive one.

Happiness is connected etymologically, and in reality, with the word "happen." It is always part of a "happening" in life which comes and goes. Only a fool expects to find happiness continually, or to hold onto it once found. Happiness is always a by-product of some feeling or action. Even knowing this, there are many of us who spend our lives frantically *looking for happiness,* constantly in mad pursuit of *joy.* We complain that our relationships are dull. We act as if these things are to be found *out there somewhere.* We seldom come to terms with the idea that happiness is in *us.* Soren Kierkegaard recognizing that when "a man, who as a physical being is always turned toward the outside, thinking that his happiness lies outside him, finally turns inward and discovers that the source is within him," is one of life's great insights.

We cannot look for joy as we do a lost article of clothing. We make our own happiness. We define it for ourselves and experience it in our unique way. No one can be happy for us nor tell us what should make us happy, though people will always try. The sad fact is that we fall into Madison Avenue traps which convince us that happiness is the right drink, the flashy automobile, the scented deodorant, bursting-with-health cereal or the special snack food. Even the wisest among us are seduced by the exuberant TV ad or the seductive graphic into believing that we, too, can change our lives if we switch to a new mouthwash. We never stop to think that there is nothing in the world which can be given or denied us that will bring us happiness unless we decide it. In fact, the happiest people in the world would probably still be happy if stripped of everything except life.

I recall when I was travelling through Asia that I was constantly encountering people who existed, according to our standards, at barely above a starvation level, yet they lived in genuine joy. Their lives were filled with smiles, song, dance and celebration of whatever they had. Of course, I am not advocating the naive illusion of the "happy peasant." All who so desire should be able to rise above whatever social condition in which they were born and attain whatever prize they want for what they believe to be their betterment or happiness. What I'm saying is that nothing but *life itself* is necessary for humans to know joy and happiness.

I constantly had this affirmed in my work with handicapped individuals. I saw quadriplegics who smiled and laughed their way through life, while those working with them, with every physical advantage, were often miserable, unsatisfied and depressed. It is strange that some of the happiest people I have ever known were those who seemed to have no particular cause to rejoice. They were simply happy. They seemed to have in common a singular courage, a willingness to risk, to fail and to let go, a belief in themselves, a wonderful resourcefulness, a trust in their creative uniqueness and an ability to hold on to their dream.

Perhaps much happiness is lost in the pursuit of it. Hawthorne in his *American Notebooks* said that happiness always comes incidentally. "Make it the object of pursuit," he stated, "and it leads us on a wild goose chase and is never attained." He suggests that we should lose our way and follow something totally unrelated. In that way we often happen on happiness without ever dreaming it would be there.

We are far too rational in our relationships, far too ordered, organized and predictable. We need to find a place, just this side of madness and irrationality, where we can, from time to time, leave the mundane and move into spontaneity and serendipity, a level that includes a greater sense of freedom and risk — an active environment full of surprises, which encourages a sense of wonder. Here, ideas and feelings which would otherwise be difficult to state can be expressed freely. A bond of love is easy to find in an environment of joy. When we laugh together we bypass reason and logic, as the clown does. We speak a universal language. We feel closer to one another.

Joy, humor, laughter — all are wonderful, easily accessible tools for bringing comfort into a relationship. They can be used to overcome inhibitions and tension. Dr. William Fry of Stanford University has just recently reported that laughter aids digestion (give up your antacids), stimulates the heart and strengthens muscles (give up jogging), and activates the brain's creative function and keeps you alert (give up artificial stimulants). All this with a good guffaw.

Joy and happiness are simply states of mind. As such

they can help us to find creative solutions. When we feel joyful, euphoric, happy, we are more open to life, more capable of seeing things clearly and handling daily tensions. When one laughs, the body secretes a special hormone that is a natural painkiller. Norman Cousins claims to have cured himself of a terminal illness with, among other things, the power of laughter. Good uproarious laughter of the roll-in-the-aisle type, causes all the vital organs to vibrate and jostle, much like what happens to us when we jog. So, if we are too lazy to jog, we can laugh our way to health! Throw out the aspirin and giggle away despair.

For years, I had been told that I was taking life too casually, that my attitude would surely lead me to wrack and ruin. A man of my professional background should be an example — firm, serious, with his "feet planted firmly on the ground." With my two feet "firmly planted on the ground," I found I couldn't get my pants on! With my feet in the air, it's easier now!

"Joy comes in our lives," Joseph Addison says, "when we have something to do, something to love, and something to hope for."

Live fully and with abandon. Love totally and without fear. Hope splendidly and never relinquish the dream. These will help us but joy will only be ours when we choose it. As Abraham Lincoln reminded us, "Most folks are about as happy as they make up their minds to be."

Many a relationship has been saved by a good belly laugh.

CHAPTER 6

Loving Each Other Enough To Let Go : Jealousy

I thought that jealousy was an idea. It isn't. It's a pain. But I didn't feel as they do in a Broadway melodrama. I didn't want to kill anybody. I just wanted to die.

FLOYD DELL

Jealousy is delightful during courtship, practically essential to the first year of marriage, but after that, Chinese torture.

SECUDES, 1957

"I'll kill him!" she told me. "I love him so much I'd rather see him dead than with another woman!" A strange, illogical response, or a very human one? A dictionary definition can, in no way, begin to describe that desperate cluster of feelings we have characterized as jealousy. Powerful and universal as they are, few of us are prepared or equipped to handle them when they suddenly — often without warning — overtake us. This emotion has the power to overwhelm and destroy the most seemingly sound and secure relationship, the most rational person. A lost handkerchief was sufficient cause to madden Othello enough to murder Desdemona, his faithful and loving wife. Jason's love of another woman was sufficient reason to cause Medea to kill their children in violent revenge! We need not look to history and mythology for such examples. Our newspapers report them daily.

At some time or another most all of us have known jealousy. It is no respecter of social position, intellectual or economic level, or age. I remember the uncomfortable, self-defeating, rather frightening feeling, even as a child. I had a most lovable dog, Queeny, who was given to me on my seventh birthday. She was a gift to *me*. She was full of love, eager to receive it and generous about sharing it with everyone. I was livid over the attention she showered upon others. No one had *taught* me to be jealous; still, I was; and it pained me beyond belief. After all, wasn't that attention rightfully and exclusively mine? I bathed her, fed her, cleaned up after her. She was *mine*. I felt her wanton attention to others was a direct threat to me. How dare she! I felt self-righteous and, at the same time, ashamed. I felt all-powerful, but knew I was helpless. I thought rationally, but behaved irrationally. I knew that I could not stop Queeny from loving others, that it did not detract from her love for me, but it didn't help. My feeling vacillated between love and hate. I was overwhelmed with the desire to control and possess. It took a great deal of time for me to realize that in her unwavering love for all, little Queeny was free; I, in my greed, was a prisoner.

Jealousy is a universal feeling. It isn't sick or pathological until it is acted upon. The feeling is normal. The behavior it elicits is what is often irrational.

Feelings of jealousy are not always bad. It is often through such feelings that we acquire the necessary insight which causes us to appreciate the value of another person. Jealous feelings can also serve to bring our neurotic needs to the surface and thus cause us to change our behavior. Sigmund Freud suggested that "Jealousy is one of those affective states, like grief, that may be described as normal." In fact, he believed that those who felt they were totally free of jealous feelings were probably deluding themselves or simply repressing their feelings and putting them out of their conscious lives. As a result of this, Freud suggested these individu-

122

als were forced to deal with the ramifications of jealousy on an *unconscious* level of behavior. Repressed and out of conscious control, it could, at any time, emerge suddenly without warning, and in this way, be far more dangerous. Of course, Freud was not suggesting that extremes of jealousy — delusion and pathological forms — were normal. He, as well as other students of jealousy, felt it important to stress that though we all to some degree know the feeling, it becomes pathological when we refuse to deal with it in rational ways.

Jealousy can be either good or bad, not so much depending upon what we feel, but what we do and how we act upon what we feel. Jealousy doesn't exist in a vacuum. It is mainly aroused in active, loving relationships with others. Often, the more we care, the greater the possibility of jealousy. Relationships generally begin in a mutual attraction. As this attraction grows, it often suggests possession. We segregate each other from the masses. We talk joyfully of *my* girlfriend, *my* boyfriend, *my* wife, *my* family, *my* baby, *my* co-workers. The closer we move to each other, the more we willingly assume responsibility for each other. We eagerly listen to one another's history and observe each other's patterns of behavior. We meet the other's friends and family. We share concerns, fears, decisions, patterns of action and responses. In other words, we assume a greater investment in each other as unique, separate individuals. We eagerly devise to move from an "I" and "me" to a new, more valued unit, which we see as "us" and "we." We dedicate time and energy to those things which will further define and enhance that new unit. We revel in "our song," "our restaurant," "our shared experience," our special names of endearment for each other. We strive to continually merge together as one. We share our beliefs, our opinions, our loyalties, our trust.

In attempting to accomplish these complex and subtle behaviors, without guaranteed security or permanence, we are always susceptible to the possibilities of jealousy. "He is late getting home from the office." "She is making too many new friends." "They are excluding me." Any threat to "our" newly-created dream can bring on a fear of loss and a sense of panic over the possibility of losing the good that we have created. Only we can suffer our loss, we are left alone in our struggle with seemingly no one to turn to. There is no one who can really understand our pain, our panic, our fear. We may even rationally know that these feelings are unfounded. In our shame we cannot explain them to others. Alone, bitter and helpless, it is natural that we begin to direct the blame for our pain outward toward someone other than ourselves. Surely we are not the cause of this. It is *their* behavior that is responsible for it. It is *they* who have betrayed us, who have shaken the security of the relationship, who have brought ruin to the wonderful world we had together. It is always the other's fault. The failure of our "we" is never our failure. Alone, we grope for some support system. We often find this by shifting the blame to others.

Beecher in *The Mark of Cain* states:

> They are given to pointing the finger of blame *outside* themselves at some other person as if that person were responsible for their discomfort and their feelings of inadequacy. No one, of course, is ever destroyed by

another person in this sense. A jealous individual, or any disturbed individual, is destroyed only from *inside himself.*

Jealousy can be handled in many ways. Perhaps the most instinctive response, when security or possession is threatened, is aggression — to fight for what we believe is rightfully ours. Some of us rationalize. We tell ourselves that the other person is inferior to us. We convince ourselves that we are above the situation, that it is just too trivial to deal with. By doing these things, we are sometimes able to temporarily lessen the pain. Others are able to repress these sensations altogether. The human psyche is an amazing thing. Often we can so completely bury our feelings that they appear to be nonexistent. At least for a while.

Others choose to withdraw. They escape the situation by convincing themselves that what they don't know can't hurt them. Still others move away from the situation, believing that the closer they are to the source of pain, the more pain they will experience, that the further away they are, the more likely it is that the pain will lessen.

There are those who will enjoy playing the martyr. They will suffer in silence, dying a thousand painful deaths a day. They feel helpless but do nothing about it. They wait, they hope, they pray for things to get better.

Some play the sadist. They scream and accuse and threaten and fight. They narrow their lips and furrow their brows and swear that they will get even. They seek ways to hurt the one they once loved so deeply. They are determined to "get back" at them and show them that "two can play at that game."

Though some of the above ploys seem to work for some people some of the time, most of us find these but temporary reliefs from the hopeless, helpless feelings that jealousy can arouse. Even drowning these feelings in alcohol, drugs, casual encounters and wild parties, prove but transient solutions; and, after the brief respite is over, we are left with our emptiness and anger unresolved.

Since few of us who choose to form relationships with others will be totally free of jealousy, perhaps it would be best to look at better, more lasting ways to come to terms with the emotion. The great psychoanalyst/philosopher Theodore Reich has said, "Jealousy is a sign that something is wrong, not necessarily rotten, in the organism of love." Perhaps seeing jealousy as a warning of "something wrong" is the first positive step to its being corrected, since to fight or try to negate jealousy doesn't actually solve anything. The only real solution to jealousy seems to be to work it out. Feeling a strong emotion is necessary to making changes. Anthropologist Margaret Mead has suggested that jealousy is an emotion which is "a festering spot in every personality so affected, an ineffective, negativistic attitude which is more likely to lose than gain any goal." But, she admits that it may be of value for it may be responsible for the passion, the intensity, from which is born enterprise. In her anthropological studies of the people of Samoa she found no jealousy, but she also found few strong feelings, competition, or motivation.

We are responsible for our jealousy, no one else. Blaming others for what we feel, can lead nowhere. Change will only begin when we are willing to accept our jealousy as our responsibility, not necessarily bad unless negatively acted upon. Relieving others of our responsibility, we can then begin the productive processes necessary for finding out what can be done about it.

Rollo May, the famous analyst, has said:

> Jealousy requires turning one's attention to one's self and asking why is my self-esteem so low in the first place? I quite understand that this question may be difficult to answer. But at least it turns your concern to an area you can do something about.

Persons who cling to jealousy destroy *themselves*. They use energies for dead-end feelings which could be channeled into creative solutions. Of course, no one chooses to be jealous, it simply happens. What is essential is to change the values and beliefs which created the response. Jealousy generates much feeling, but actually produces little action. It becomes an insidious process which keeps us from seeing accurately what there is. It nurtures only itself. It succeeds only in making us feel impotent. As such, jealousy is most often a product of our personal insecurity and low self-esteem. It occurs because we see ourselves as having less to give than the object of our jealousy. It steals our rationality. We become unable to see our strengths and allow ourselves to be overcome by what we are convinced are weaknesses and inadequacies. We feel valueless. We lose our sense of dignity and worth. We become frenzied, paralyzed or afraid to act. We forget the simple fact that because someone does not elect to meet whatever conditions have been imposed in our relationship, our true inner value as a person is not diminished, nor is theirs.

We forget that we cannot force anyone to meet our needs, to be what we want them to be, do what we want them to do, respond as we would have them respond or feel what we think they should feel. This is a human impossibility, an illusion, a fantasy. Even if the other person concedes to being "ours," at best that is only a figure of speech.

Perhaps we must finally accept the fact that we can never possess another human being. A decision to unite is an agreement between two separate units, which will always, in a sense, be separate. We must learn that loving others is to want them to be themselves — painful as it may be — with or without you. After all is said and done, what else can we do but wish them well? If a friend or loved one wants to go, even if we devise a hundred ways to try to hold on, we will never be successful. And how little we value ourselves when we manipulate someone in order to keep them, when they would rather be elsewhere. We are better without those individuals in our lives.

Jealousy diminishes only when we regain a feeling of worth and self-respect, stop internalizing the problem and begin to view it objectively as something stemming from our personal demands and needs. These may arise from our desire for status or loyalty. They may be due to our insecurity, our need to control, to possess, our need for exclusivity, or fear of loss of face.

Loyalty in a relationship is based upon trust and respect. It can only be offered, never demanded. It is based upon voluntary devotion. Relationships are continually changing. A mutual agreement to be loyal or honest will form the basis from which future trust will arise. Loyalty is, therefore, a pact. Fidelity is a pact. The earlier these qualities are discussed and agreed upon in a relationship, the more secure the future of the relationship. Of course, the decision must be mutual, and the decision must be binding. Any change in the expectations over time must be accepted, discussed, and new decisions formed.

The word "jealousy" stems from the Greek word "jeal." It suggests that a valued possession is in danger and that some action must be taken. It implies that what can be seen as a negative phenomenon can be changed to a positive one over time. As the relationship, and those involved in it, becomes stronger and more secure, so will jealousy be minimized. Learning to let go, since most of us believe that love is based on "holding on to," is very difficult. Perhaps the greatest love presupposes the greatest freedom. There is an old saying which suggests that love must be set free, and when it comes back to you, only then will you know real love.

When we have finally conquered extremes of jealousy, we will emerge better and stronger lovers. We will understand the joy and strength which comes from solving our own problems, meeting our own needs, and loving freely without demands. As always after having conquered something of a lower order, we will be lifted to new and greater heights.

Eleanor Roosevelt said:

> Every time you meet a situation, though you think at the time it is an impossibility and you go through the tortures of the damned, once you have met it and lived through it, you find that forever after you are freer than you were before.

Don't be afraid of jealousy. It is a natural and normal

emotion. Everyone who cares and loves feels jealous at one time or another. The essential decision is whether you will allow your jealousy to become an all-consuming monster, capable of destroying you and those you love, or become a challenge for you to grow in self-respect and personal knowledge. The challenge will rest with you.

CHAPTER 7

Loving
Each Other
In Intimacy

*The moment we indulge our affections,
the earth is metamorphosed.*

EMERSON

*Talk not of wasted affection. Affection
never was wasted.*

LONGFELLOW

She was looking down, rather sadly, at her purse when she said, plaintively, "I know my husband can be affectionate and tender. He's that way with the dog!"

With the dog! As many know, I make it a point, after every public lecture, to mingle with the audience. This offers us a time for general exchanges of joy, greetings and friendly hugs. At each lecture I encounter at least one person, attractive, often elderly, who will whisper as we embrace, "You're the first man who has hugged me since my husband died seven years ago!" I meet men who confess to not having hugged another man, even their own sons, since they were children. "It feels good," they often say. One man I particularly remember, sighed, "It's like going home again."

Parents and teachers too often touch children only when pushing, pulling or directing them about. This is so, even though it has been clearly demonstrated that there is a direct relationship between the degree of physical closeness children experience and their physical and mental health.

Most of us never embrace fully, even those we love. Interestingly, we seem to reserve our embraces for sexual acts, for moments when we have just won a TV jackpot or for tragic moments in our lives in hospital rooms or at funerals.

The need for physical closeness seems to become most apparent at times of catastrophe. After earthquakes, floods and severe accidents, we rush desperately to seek security in the arms of another human being. It is interesting that men who would never do so otherwise, after a highly successful athletic feat, jump wildly into each other's arms, pat each other on the backside and kiss in abandoned glee.

It is natural for us to want to show affection. But for some mysterious reason, we equate tenderness with sentimentality, weakness and vulnerability. We seem to be as fearful to give it as to receive it. Desmond Morris in his outstanding work, *Intimate Behavior,* states that this belief causes us to . . .

> . . . arrive at a state in which all contact seems repellent, where to touch or to be touched means to hurt or be hurt. This, in a sense, has become one of the greatest ailments of our time, a major social disease of modern society that we would be well to cure before it is too late. If the danger remains unheeded then — like poisonous chemicals in our food — it may increase from generation to generation until the damage has gone beyond repair.

Fortunately, in spite of ourselves, most of us unconsciously touch daily. We shake hands, we pat each other on the back, we playfully mess each other's hair, or more formally, we hold each other as we dance. These all represent common, physical, nonsexual expressions of affection. They are very human ways of bringing others closer, expressing our love and understanding or conveying our warmth. They are simple human acts. Still, for some of us they present monumental barriers.

134

The popular psychiatrist, Harold Bloomfield, in his book, *Making Peace with Your Parents,* recounts the story of how he was unable to hug his father until he found that his father was dying of cancer. They had to relearn the process from an awkward embrace to one that ended with a true expression of "I love you." The embrace healed Dr. Bloomfield and gave new life to his father, mother and entire family.

I recall a classic Italian film by the eminent director Antonioni in which the protagonists were in the process of breaking a long-lasting and what was once a loving relationship. The lover is in tears, despondent, sitting with his head buried in his hands, unable to speak. His girlfriend knows she has only to touch him gently on the shoulder to bring him out of this helpless, hopeless state. She tries several times, but it is as if her hand weighs too much to consummate the act. She finally picks up her purse and scarf and quietly leaves the room. The scene was chilling.

These behaviors have always been difficult for me to understand. I recall the confusion I had as a child, coming from a very affectionate family, when I learned that other children did not sit on their parents' laps to be caressed, nor did they hug and kiss family and guests at the drop of a hat. I used to hug my classmates who said I was "queer." Even my teachers told me that the rule was "Hands off! We don't do that in this country." I remember replying defensively, "We do in my house." "Well, not in my classroom!" was the final word.

Even now, my natural tendency is to open my arms to others when we meet. This is considered by many who

don't know me to be a rather shocking approach, or
simply a gimmick. Thus, the frivolous title, "Dr. Hug."
Others respond as if it is an invasion of their privacy.
Judith Martin, who writes on etiquette under the name,
Miss Manners, actually asked me not to touch her. She
said she only allowed her husband and King Louis XIV
to touch her. In the end I hugged her anyway, hoping that
she received sufficient hugs from her husband, knowing
that it was too late for Louis XIV. I recall a popular TV
interviewer who cautioned me prior to a show that he
wasn't a hugger so, "Hands off, I'm a man," he said,
"and I don't want my viewers to think I'm queer." On
the other hand, many others including Phil Donahue,
Diane Sawyer, and Hugh Downs have been most recep-
tive to a human hug. A very sincere man in the audience
of a Donahue show on which I was appearing, was
genuinely upset that my advocacy of "hugging" would
create a country of sexual perverts.

Desmond Morris suggests that the fear of touching
was related to old, often unconscious, sexual taboos.
This idea has made it extremely difficult for us to indulge
in any physical contact without the implication of sexual
involvement. He states that this has resulted in

> . . . a massive inhibition of our nonsexual body inti-
> macies and this has applied to relationships with our
> parents and offspring (beware, Oedipus!), our siblings
> (beware, incest!), our close same-sex friends (beware,
> homosexuality!), our close opposite-sex friends
> (beware, adultery), and our many casual friends
> (beware, promiscuity). All of this is understandable but
> totally unnecessary.

In point of fact, it has been shown that our ability to

become emotionally involved with others, to learn to trust and to become vulnerable to loving and being loved, is directly related to our experiences of having been stroked, caressed and cuddled as children. We learn affection from the tender models in our lives. We learn security by feeling the warmth of being held in moments of need. We learn tenderness through gentle experiences with others. From the moment of conception, the emerging infant is softly enveloped in the warmth and embrace of the womb. After birth, so essential is the continuance of this security that a child left untouched and uncuddled, will form a bonding relationship with anything present, even stuffed toys and surrogate mother apes. If all human tactile experiences are denied, the child will die.

A simple caress has the potential of changing a whole life. The warm embrace, withheld at the vital moment when it is most desperately needed, can easily be the act, or rather the non-act, that finally destroys a relationship, or even a nation!

Our physical needs continue for our lifetime and no amount of cultural restriction or sophistication can succeed in dispelling them. We have unwritten taboos on touching. We are often shocked when we travel to Europe, Africa or Asia to find people hugging, leaning against each other, holding hands, forever engaging in human contact.

Helen Colton, in her interesting and challenging book, *The Gift of Touch,* tells of numerous experiments with touching which have revealed emotional and intellectual benefits. She writes of a social scientist who did an observational study of touching habits of Americans versus Parisians. In an hour's time the experimentor found that European friends touched each other at least 100 times while Americans touched each other no more than three or four times.

Our ability to relate will be largely determined by our experience with touch from the beginning of our lives. It is certainly true that no one would expect a mother, for instance, to indulge in as much physical behavior with an adolescent or young adult as she would with an infant. Affection needs change in degree and kind at different times. But demonstrated affection is necessary for health at all stages. The degree of caring about another, in fact, can be measured by the amount of time and energy we dedicate to physical availability. It is natural that we want to be close to those we love.

Our actual body chemistry changes when we are physically close to another. As the body automatically adjusts to threatening situations by pumping more adrenaline into the bloodstream causing us to make life-saving decisions to turn and run, to fight, to attack or whatever, so it does with closeness. If we have learned to be suspect of or fear closeness, it will produce the same response as do threatening situations and we will crave distance. Our intimacy behaviors are conditioned. If we are fearful of closeness, we will run from it or learn to create safe distances. But, also, as we learn the joy of closeness, our body responds in kind with general feelings of well-being, relaxation, security, tenderness, fearlessness and we continue to move toward others.

Harold Lyon in his book *Tenderness is Strength* says,

> We have lost sight of the fact that we human beings are, in one respect, like small animals without even any fur

or sharp teeth to protect us. What protects us is not our viciousness, but our humanity; our ability to love others and to accept the love that others want to offer us. It is not our toughness that keeps us warm at night, but our tenderness which makes others want to keep us warm.

Studies have continually revealed that the need to be touched is innate in all warm-blooded animals. Contact causes them to feel more comfortable and peaceful. Touch deprivation, on the other hand, often leads to despondency, loss of appetite, apathy and a decline in efficient functioning. Dr. Harold Voth, psychiatrist at the Menninger Foundation in Kansas, has said,

Hugging can lift depression — enabling the body's immune system to become tuned up. Hugging breathes fresh life into a tired body and makes you feel younger and more vibrant. In the home, daily hugging will strengthen relationships and significantly reduce friction.

Helen Colton reinforces this with research which indicates that,

. . . when a person is touched, the amount of hemoglobin in the blood increases significantly. Hemoglobin is a part of the blood that carries vital supplies of oxygen to all organs of the body — including the heart and brain. An increase in hemoglobin tones up the whole body, helps prevent disease and speeds recovery from illness.

Dr. Voth and Ms. Colton recommend that you hug your spouse, your children, close friends or relatives often. "If you live alone," Dr. Voth suggests, "the warm embrace of a friend whenever you meet is just as beneficial. It's a marvelous way to improve the quality of your life."

While director of the Pain Control Unit at UCLA, Dr. David Bresler wrote,

> We can all benefit by learning to express and meet our physical needs in a loving, caressing way. Thus, I give many of my patients a homework assignment: During the upcoming weeks, they are to get and give four hugs a day. I even write out a formal prescription that says simply, "Four hugs a day — without fail." Don't ever underestimate how powerful this therapy can be, and the role it can play in the healing process. And it's a safe prescription, too. To my knowledge, no one has ever died of an overdose of hugging. However, as one of my patients told me, "It is addicting. Once you start hugging, it's a hard habit to break!"

The Columbus Dispatch of January 16, 1983, reported on an Ohio State University study of the correlation of a high fat diet and arteriosclerosis in test rabbits. The study showed that rabbits on the same high fat diet who were picked up and held by students had only half as much fatty deposit building in blood vessels as the others. "Perhaps this explains to a small degree why so many more men than women have arteriosclerosis," concluded the study.

Helen Colton tells us of studies by Jack Pankaepp of Bowling Green State University in Ohio, which suggest a positive relationship between adolescents who use drugs and those who come from homes in which there is little or no touching. She also relates a study by James Prescott who found a positive correlation between the degree of violence and cruelty within 30 cultures and the amount of tactile, sensory contact within each culture.

Whether or not these studies are fully valid, there is no denying that touching confers healthful benefits. Still we remain a tactilely undernourished society. Desmond Morris says,

> Unhappily, and almost without noticing it, we have gradually become less and less touchful, more and more distant, and physical untouchability has been accompanied by emotional remoteness. It is as if the modern urbanite has put on a suit of emotional armor and, with a velvet hand inside an iron glove, is beginning to feel trapped and alienated from the feelings of even his nearest companions.

Teenagers admit that the lack of tenderness in their lives often leads them to promiscuous behaviors. They become, interestingly enough, "a soft touch." They will do things which are totally out of character and outside the perimeters of their value systems in order to be held in warmth and acceptance.

Human sexuality, which is, perhaps, the most significant show of deeply felt closeness, has, over the years, lost its relationship to affection. We seldom talk about "making love" — rather we refer to it as "having sex" or "making out" and other, more crude, expressions. Sexuality and loving intimacy are not necessarily synonyms, though not mutually exclusive. Sexuality can be totally divorced from any semblance of love. It can be simply an act of genital satisfaction. It may be exclusive of any concern for the individual or the perpetuation of the species. The body of one human being is used to satisfy the need of another, no more. It may have little or nothing to do with love or tenderness or caring or sharing or pleasing. It is merely an act of copulation satisfying a need. Without the essential ingredient, the expression of love and affection, the sex act is totally devoid of primary benefits such as prolonged security and satisfaction; this can be achieved only in complete physical and emotional union. Like any drug, sex without love becomes simply an expression of basic physical need and personal desire and wears off as soon as orgasm is achieved, accomplishing nothing toward prolonged relating or loving.

The literature over the past ten years has been replete with implications that the major cause of unsatisfying relationships among adults is the lack of sexual knowledge or technique. The result has been the endless production of best-selling volumes of sexual manuals. These run the gamut from vividly illustrated books to scientific, detailed explanations of the "G" spot or the "total" orgasm. We are told that without an understanding of these phenomena, relationships will suffer, will be incomplete and that love is impossible. Uta West, in her book, *If Love is the Answer, What is the Question?* tells of a debate on love and orgasm between the authors James Baldwin and Norman Mailer. Baldwin questioned the relevancy of orgasm to love and told Mailer that, in the ghettos where he grew up, "men and women had orgasms all the time, and still cut each other up with razors on Saturday nights."

In *One to One,* Dr. Theodore Rubin says that the emphasis on technique and sexual misinformation,

> . . . are destructive to the sexual health of any relationship and lead to dissatisfaction and disturbance between would-be relating lovers. Undue emphasis on concrete mechanical (sexual) expertise; performance anxiety; stereotyping of 'ideal' lovers as well as of

'ideal' response, all these things have diluted the connection between sex and affection.

This has led more than one person to feel that rather than an expression of love, sex has become a skill or an exercise. "I'm so tense during sexual intercourse, deciding if I'm doing it right — I seldom feel anything at all," a friend confessed.

Dr. Rubin speaks to this feeling when he says,

> This stress on mechanics is destructive. It leads to superficialities and to pride investment in performance rather than to healthy interest in richer relating. Sexual athletics simply do not provide long-lasting or deeper satisfactions, and to expect them to do so is asking for disappointment — disappointment that is destructive to all areas of the relationship.

The psychiatrist Rollo May, in his classic, *Love and Will,* affirms this view. He says,

> A second paradox is that the new emphasis on technique in sex and love-making backfires. It often occurs to me that there is an inverse relationship between the number of how-to-do-it books perused by a person or rolling off the presses in a society and the amount of sexual passion or even pleasure experienced by the persons involved. Certainly nothing is wrong with technique as such, in playing golf or acting or making love. But the emphasis beyond a certain point on technique in sex makes for a mechanistic attitude toward love-making and goes along with alienation, feelings of loneliness and depersonalization.

I am almost certain that if one loves another enough, he or she will discover position 63 or the Z or G or Q spot without a guidebook. I am not suggesting that ignorance is the best policy, only that the preoccupation with mechanics of intimacy can be detrimental to the essence of true affection which should be a spontaneous physical celebration of the deepest form of togetherness. The latest research coming from studies of individuals choosing to experiment with cohabitation rather than marriage has affirmed this. It has been found that these arrangements, entered into as a type of noncommittal, pseudo-intimacy to overcome loneliness and afford the couple easy sexual access, are more satisfying to men than they are to women. Incompatible sexuality is often given as the reason for the dissolutions of these relationships — but it has been found that it is more closely related to the fear of true commitment and deep intimacy. In these relationships, the essence is to have it all — and commitment is avoided. It becomes, therefore, but a caricature of an intimate relationship and in no way can it determine the success or failure of the relationship once true commitment is added.

I have not meant to minimize the joy or value of a stimulating and exciting sex life. I have meant only to stress that sexuality is a vital part of a relationship but in no way is it the *only* or even the *most important* show of affection. Still, it is interesting to note that in the mounds of materials I perused relating to intimacy, almost all of it related to affection and closeness in heterosexual relationships. Family intimacy, homosexual intimacy and nonsexual intimacy were almost totally absent. It may be true that the famous loves in history have been between members of the opposite sex; but historically, the deepest friendships have always been between those of the same sex. Yet the literature on the most universal experience of all, the deep nonsexual affection to be found in friendship, is all but nonexistent.

I know that there are many who will respond to the above with strong negative feelings. "I don't want to be touched!" they say. "I want my privacy. Hands off." Certainly, I appreciate their attitude. They obviously feel uncomfortable with physical shows of affection. There are certainly many varied ways to express closeness. Perhaps these individuals have found their personal methods for satisfying intimacy needs. It is hoped they have.

It is not easy to change old habits. If we are strangers to the physical show of affection, it is natural that it will create anxiety and discomfort in us. But if we feel touch-starved and a need to change our physically intimate behavior, then it is well to know that it can be done. But as with all behavioral change, we should not expect that it will happen overnight. To start embracing, after years of standing aloof, would be unnatural. We may want to start making contact within the safety of family and caring, understanding friends. We may want them to verbally express our need and desire to change our touching behaviors. We may want to start with a hand-shake, a pat on the back, a touch of the fingers, and move to other more intimate, nonsexual behavior such as a warm hug or a tender kiss on the cheek. The results are often immediate and dramatic. Most of us have had enough of estrangement. We have a need to find new closeness, new ways to come together, to bridge gaps with those we love. Of course, physical closeness is but one way of communicating ourselves. It is this communication which is a vital element for creating relationships.

The idea of warmth, touch, tenderness and caring is portrayed powerfully in a poem called *Minnie Remembers* by Donna Swanson. It appears in her book titled *Mind Song*. I share it here.

> How long has it been since someone touched me? Twenty years I've been a widow. Respected. Smiled at. But never touched. . . . . Oh God, I'm so lonely. I remember Hank and the babies. How else can I remember them but together? Hank didn't seem to mind if my body thickened and faded a little. He loved it and he loved to touch it. And the children hugged me, a lot. . . . . Oh God, I'm lonely! God, why didn't we raise the kids to be silly and affectionate as well as dignified and proper. They drive up in their fine cars. They come to my room to pay their respects. They chatter brightly and reminisce. But they don't touch me. They call me Mom, or Mother or Grandma. Never Minnie. My mother called me Minnie. So did my friends. Hank called me Minnie, too. But they're gone. And so is Minnie.

Minnie is not a stranger to most of us, sad to say. We continue to be a culture of mostly well-clothed, overfed and pampered individuals. We have so much. Still, we suffer from one of the most dangerous deprivations — the inability to express our love with open and honest affection and without fear. It takes so little to open our arms one to the other. It is one of the clearest and most expansive statements we can make.

CHAPTER 8

Loving Each Other: Some Solicited Advice

Never give advice. The ignorant won't heed it and the wise don't need it.

THE WASHINGTON POST

I have never been keen on advice. I firmly believe that the best answers for each of us are already in us. All we need to do to realize these is to recognize them and act upon them.

When I was preparing the relationships questionnaire, I kept thinking of the years of experience in loving that we could profit from if I were to ask the participants to offer a bit of "Solicited Advice." Many of the respondents said they did not give advice, even solicited. But the majority were willing to offer some ideas which they felt might be of help. It was my feeling that their ideas were well worth sharing. If the respondents included the same suggestions as in the major part of the questionnaire, they are not repeated here.

The following comments added, to my mind, some thoughtful material to be pondered even by the most sophisticated among us. They reflect a genuine and down-to-earth quality that can't help but be of value.

Don't think in terms of forever. Think of now, and forever will take care of itself.

Grow up together, constantly.

Expect to invest a great deal of time and energy in your relationships. Lasting relationships don't just happen, they are created.

Recognize that all relationships cannot be forever. Recognize their temporary quality, but continue to act as if they are permanent.

Respect the other person's relationships apart from you. If they are important to the one you care about, they should be important to you.

Never idealize others. They will never live up to your expectations.

Take your time.

Remove price tags from people. Everyone has worth; the excitement lies in the discovery of their value.

Don't be afraid of giving. You can never give too much, if you're giving willingly.

Don't feel as if you are required to spend your every waking hour with those you love. Move aside from time to time and allow them a separate space, too.

Never force anyone to do anything for you "in the name of love." Love is not to be bargained for.

Don't be afraid.

Don't over analyze your relationships.

Realize that you always have choices. It's up to you.

Remember that a relationship is a pooling of resources. That means that with each relationship you are not only giving, you are becoming more.

Don't allow experience to harden your heart; rather use it to become more aware and sensitive.

Don't smother each other. No one can grow in shade.

Don't lose touch with the craziness in you. This, with a large dose of caring, will assure that your relationship will never be boring.

Don't brood. Get on with living and loving. You don't have forever.

Don't hold on to anger, hurt or pain. They steal your energy and keep you from love.

Always start a relationship by asking: Do I have ulterior motives for wanting to relate to this person? Is my caring conditional? Am I trying to escape something? Am I planning to change the person? Do I need this person to help me make up for a deficiency in myself? If your answer to any of these questions is "Yes," leave the person alone. He or she is better off without you.

There are times when you may want to give up on a relationship, but never give up on relating.

Keep the child in you alive and playing.

See people as good and beautiful, even when they seem to be trying hard not to appear so.

_____

If you take time to talk together each day you'll never become strangers.

_____

Divorce, fighting, arguing will never solve your problems; better to try understanding, warmth and flexibility.

_____

Value yourself. The only people who appreciate a doormat are people with dirty shoes.

Stop going through life in self-pity, self-blame and the "mea culpa" syndrome. We are not as bad as we think.

Before you form a relationship, ask yourself if there are things about the other that you can't stand. If there are, ask yourself if you would be able to live with these things forever. If the answer is "no," then leave it alone.

Write down all the reasons why you love each person you relate with. Then, when the going gets tough, take the list out and reread it. It resolves problems quickly.

Don't make the other's problems yours. It only makes solving it twice as difficult.

Don't be afraid of disagreements and arguments, the only people who don't argue are people who don't care or are dead. In fact, don't have short arguments. Make certain they are thoroughly over and done with.

After an argument is over, forget it.

Learn to bend. It's better than breaking.

Don't take yourself so seriously, but never fail to take the other person seriously.

Don't become involved in pettiness, ego and childish hurts. These will only serve to degrade your relationships and prevent closeness.

Watch for little irritations, they grow into destructive monsters. Verbalize them at once.

Let go of pride. It is usually false, creates barriers and prevents closeness.

Acknowledge the humanness of the other.

___

Keep examining the nature of each of your relationships for they are dynamic, not static, and are, therefore, changing for better or worse.

___

Exercise feelings. Feelings have meaning only as they are expressed in action.

___

Increase tenderness and intimacy. They are a powerful source of nourishment to relationships.

Be compassionate. It is the sure way to understanding and acceptance.

See all criticism as positive for it leads to self-evaluation. You are always free to reject it if it is unfair or does not apply.

Learn to listen. You don't learn anything from hearing yourself talk.

Be compassionate. It is the sure way to understanding and acceptance.

Stop all the worry. Most of what you are worried about you'll have difficulty remembering a week later.

Expect what is reasonable, not what is perfect.

If each partner in a relationship is willing to give 75% of him or her self, then you will have 50% more than you need for a perfect relationship.

Since love can be created, there is no reason to be loveless.

Don't allow anyone to put you on a pedestal. It's too easy to fall off.

Don't be concerned about what you can get from a relationship. Instead, concern yourself with what you can bring to it.

Stop playing games. A growing relationship can only be nurtured by genuineness.

Even though you are only half of a relationship, you must remain a whole person, apart from the relationship.

163

What a grand feeling to have a relationship with someone who is loved not only by you, but by many. That means you've made a good choice.

The creating of anything worthwhile takes patience and energy.

Forming good relationships takes a lot of looking. But looking can be fun.

Remember that moral and spiritual values don't restrict, they protect.

Keep laughing. It exercises your heart and protects you from cardiac problems.

Relationships are not sporting events. Stop wrestling for control. No one ever wins this kind of match except divorce lawyers.

Perhaps it's not too bad to do some things you'd rather not if it makes another happy.

What you learn about yourself will infinitely help in trying to understand others.

See problems as small miracles
which can bring about knowledge and change.

Even though maintaining your
integrity as a person, strive to
make yourself one with another.
You can do this best if you make
each one THE ONE.

Don't fall in love with love, you'll
drown in its complexities.

Be polite. Love does not give
license for rudeness.

* You are at the center of all your relationships, therefore you are responsible for your self-esteem, growth, happiness and fulfillment. Don't expect the other person to bring you these things. You must live as if you are alone and others are the gifts offered to help you to enrich your life.

When you get angry with someone it might be well to stop and consider all the things you like about them before you respond.

Don't allow your relationships to die of neglect.

CHAPTER 9

The Challenge
Of Human
Relationships

In a social environment that is ever crowded and impersonal, it is becoming increasingly important to reconsider the value of close personal relationships before we are driven to ask the forlorn question, "Whatever happened to love?"

DESMOND MORRIS

There is little doubt that most of us long for stronger, more creative and rewarding ways of loving each other. It is obvious that we can accomplish this only when we are willing to exert the necessary effort. The process will not be easy but it will be helpful if we continue to consider the following, though they may have been often stated and repeated.

Know Yourself

It does not surprise me that people feel irritated when they hear this much overused phrase, "Know yourself." The term has been tossed about since the dawn of civilization and has been especially abused over the past two decades. People offer vague general advice but very little is suggested of a specific nature as to how to bring it off. We are seldom told if we can do this alone, if one needs a guide, a psychiatrist, a minister or a mystic. Oscar Wilde said that "only the shallow know themselves." The implication of his statement is most profound. It suggests that there must never be an end to the process. There is a wonderful story of a man who emerged after years of self-study, in a state of uncontrolled elation. He ran about shouting, "I finally know! I have finally come in touch with the secret of myself. I know myself!"

A passerby stopped him in curiosity. "How wonderful," he said, "and what have you found?"

"I am one with all things," the elated man answered.

"You are one with all things?" the passerby repeated.

"You mean I'm *not*?" asked the man.

It is obvious that since we are far more potential than we shall ever be able to realize, a goal of knowing oneself fully is unrealistic. It is, at best, an ongoing process. Still, some degree of self-knowledge is essential for survival. Others can only know us to the degree to which we are known to ourselves. We must have a caring relationship with ourselves before we can expect others to do so. Since developing as a person is a lifetime process we must risk disclosing ourselves at the moment as we are — incomplete and imperfect. It is through this loving disclosure, in vulnerability, that others risk and help us to learn more about ourselves. If we place restrictions upon our relating, we will have less opportunity for learning. When we are willing to share, others will share in return. If we are afraid to disclose our imperfect selves we cannot expect others to feel secure enough to do so and we continue to remain strangers. I have a friend who assures us that he may not be much but it's all he has at the moment. This he is willing to give us. He hopes that is enough. Too often we believe that we are ready to give more, be more and adjust more than we truly are. Unless we are realistic about ourselves, there can be no true relating, no real self-growth or acceptance of others.

172

"The first affair we must consumate successfully is the love affair with ourselves," says Nathaniel Branden, in his book *The Psychology of Romantic Love.* "Only then are we ready for other love relationships." Ultimately, no matter how concerned we are about others, we must be primarily responsible for ourselves, for it is only what we have that we are able to give to another. If we feel invisible, inadequate, and victimized, then we have no power to give another visibility, security and strength.

To learn about oneself requires constant awareness of self. It suggests a commitment to the unlimited powers of the mind and body to change and grow in a volitional direction. It involves the termination of self-depreciation and self-deception and observing, as best we can, how we act out what we believe. Only those who are dedicated to knowing and accepting themselves can accept these necessary qualities in others.

Get Rid of Petty Irritants

When you consider your behavior it might be well to ask yourself, "If I were living with me, would I want to stay around?" Too often, we do not take the time to experience ourselves as others close to us do. I recall being a part of an experimental study of teachers' classroom behaviors. In this study, teachers were televised at unspecified times during the day in the classroom (without the teacher's knowledge). These tapes were to be used for self-evaluation. No one would see the TV tapes except the teacher. When they examined these films privately, most of the teachers were shocked at their behaviors. They had never seen themselves in action before. They all agreed that it was an excellent experience in self-learning. Many of us, so viewed, would probably find ourselves different from what we imagine ourselves to be. Are we complaining, demanding, thoughtless, arrogant, fault finding, insensitive, unkind, showing little respect for others, little warmth and tenderness, blaming, ordering, ridiculing, and belittling, yet seeing ourselves as loving persons? Or, is what we do and say mostly warm, loving, accepting and honest?

It is a fact that it's not the big problems that cause relationships to fail, it's a series of small things over a long period of time: little inconsiderate behaviors, thoughtless comments, small cruel acts, words left unspoken or well-intended acts that are constantly put off for a later time. Divorce records are full of what are combined together as "irreconcilable differences." If examined carefully these would boil down to being insignificant annoyances such as:

She keeps interrupting me when I talk. It drives me crazy!

He never picks up after himself.

He can't make decisions and is continually changing his mind.

She's so set in her ways. I'm afraid to touch an ashtray for fear I'll not put it back exactly where she had it. I'm less important than an ashtray!

He falls asleep in front of the TV every night. I might as well live alone.

174

He's always talking. Never says anything important. He just keeps talking.

She can't wait for me to come home to tell me in detail about every tragedy, every miserable happening.

None of these behaviors is of world-shaking importance in themselves, but allowed to continually irritate and fester, without attention, they can eventually destroy even the most secure of relationships. All of these problems can be extinguished if those concerned are willing to look at them honestly and consciously dedicate themselves to changing. Relationships fail not because they are wrong, but because most people don't want to correct their problems. They want their own way.

Bring Spontaneity and Delight Into Each Relationship

There is perhaps no greater compliment than to have people light up with joy and anticipation when you walk into a room. This happens mainly to people who bring with them an element of happiness and surprise. Most of us find that we become locked into routines which demand similar actions, responses and experiences, day after day. Surprise and serendipity have vanished as we disappear in the shadow of predictability. Many of us feel security in the belief that we can trust the familiar, that there is peace in the predictable. Actually, there is no greater trap. It is the unfamiliar, the risk, the unpredictable which potentially liberates boredom and enlivens relationships. It is the unplanned and the unknown that is rich in possibilities. Prearranged travel itineraries are perfect examples of this. We find ourselves in beautiful Capri, at an idyllic villa overlooking the azure Mediterranean. It's inexpensive. The owners are friendly, open and fun. The food is fantastic. But our itinerary says we must be in Rome tomorrow. We have tickets for the train and vouchers for hotel reservations. Alas! Of course, if we decide to live dangerously and stay on in Capri we must face the unknown — the possibility of no room in Rome, of getting on the wrong train and ending up in Abruzzi — but so what? These may be opportunities for the greatest experiences and the most extreme pleasures! I recall the madness of the young when I travelled through Europe on a Eurailpass. A group of us would stand in a station and take the first train to anywhere. It was a passage to surprise discovery and new learning! Next train to Madrid! Next train to Copenhagen! Next train to Chivasso! Istanbul! Salzburg! Oslo! London!

Of course it is not always possible to live a life in this manner. Some order, predictability and security are necessary for most of us in order to survive and maintain a sense of sanity. But a life devoid of mystery and risk is only half a life. To remain in the illusion of "security in sameness" is to miss a true understanding of what life is all about. Life was meant to be lived in surprise. In fact, in spite of ourselves, life is short; and death comes to most of us before we are ready, as the final, ultimate surprise!

Try just letting things happen from time to time. The world is full of delight if we just allow it to tell its own story without our interference.

Be Thoughtful

In authentic relating, each person is genuinely concerned for the other. This is exhibited in an active show of appreciation and regard demonstrated through words and acts of kindness, consideration and politeness. Too often we assume that closeness gives license for inconsiderate behaviors, thoughtlessness or even rudeness. It is a sad fact that we often have more concern for the feelings of casual acquaintances (even our animals) than we do for loved ones. A "thank you," "please," "I appreciate," "If you don't mind," are ways of demonstrating continued awareness and appreciation of another.

I was recently waiting in a TV news office in New York City. The space was crowded with desks, alive with ringing phones and electric with activity. If there was ever a space in need of a little human warmth and considerate behavior, this was obviously it. One of the men was so involved in his own space that he seemed totally unaware of his coworkers. He freely spat verbal abuses at them, "Where the hell were you?" "Do it now!" I wondered how long the inexcusable behavior could continue without some violent confrontation.

Too often family members forget in day-to-day interaction that they are not immune to hurt feelings. No one enjoys being put down, accused, rudely challenged, embarrassed or treated as a thing. I recall a mother who told me that she hadn't heard a "thank you" from any of her family in twelve years.

My mother always reminded us that she was our

Mama, not put on earth to be abused by us or to be our slave. To treat anyone with rudeness is to assign them a subhuman status. Mama assured us she was not subhuman and would not take rudeness from any of us. The reminder was a memorable smack on the face. Mamas need love, too.

We are frail and easily hurt. Thoughtless acts and words can, over a period of time, cut deeply through our relationships resulting in separation, unnecessary pain, tension, anger and resentment.

Each of us is responsible for creating an environment of warmth and consideration for those we love. I have always tried to define a good day not in terms of one in which all things were made right and comfortable for *me* but rather, as a day in which I have been able, through some considerate and thoughtful word or act of mine, to make another's day more loving and special for *them*. It works!

We must treat each other with dignity. Not only because we merit it but because we grow best in thoughtfulness.

Treat others with the same warmth and consideration you need and see what happens.

Stop Trying to Dominate and Change

Change is a volitional process. No one can change others without their consent. Any relationship that does not respect the individuality and choice of the other cannot survive. Closeness comes only when we have as deep a respect for the rights, attitudes and feelings of the other as we do for our own. It is well to take heed of the words of David Viscott. He writes:

> A person's individual rights in any relationship are
> the same rights he enjoyed before he even knew the
> other partner existed. Rights are not to be bargained for.
> They simply exist. A relationship's task is to recognize
> and protect the rights of both parties.

This kind of interaction comes only when we recognize others and accept them as they are without imposing our needs and expectations upon them. Each person must be allowed to stand by his or her own view of the world. Loving relating is the process of being eager to share our view by diminishing the distance between each other.

Still, many of us spend countless hours each day in the useless process of trying to make others over for our convenience. We criticize, impose guilt, manipulate in various ways, anything which will make the other person into who and what we think we need. We often do this in the name of love, certain that we know what's best for the other. We do not see this as a violation in spite of the fact that our manipulations often devalue the unique presence of the other.

If we desire to form lasting relationships with others we must start by being happy with what they are. We court disaster when we bring abusive, thoughtless and even cruel people into our lives in the assumption that under "our influence" we will make them over. Sad to say, it doesn't usually work. Change depends upon the willingness of the person to meet our needs. The only thing we can truly count upon is that we can change our behaviors in order to accommodate their abuse, thoughtlessness and cruelty.

A friend of mine was convinced that her love was

strong enough to make her very nondemonstrative husband more outwardly loving. Her husband, having been brought up in a very loving but nondemonstrative family environment, perceived compliments, tenderness, and demonstrated concern as feminine traits and felt uncomfortable in expressing them. After thirty years, my friend still feels love starved. She complains amply and bitterly to him. She calls him a "cold fish." His response is simply that she knew what she was buying when she accepted the merchandise. Even though her husband is wonderful in most other ways, she feels cheated and wronged. She remains determined to change him. She believes her relationship is a failure until she does.

Most of us are aware of what others need. In many cases they arc really asking little of us. If we truly love them then we are willing to relinquish a part of ourself for their joy. We, on the other hand, get pleasure from meeting their needs, seeing them happy and secure. The point is that behavioral change comes about volitionally. Of course, it is possible to manipulate others, to dominate them into becoming what we desire them to be. We may even create seductive environments to make this behavior fit our needs. But this seems to me to reflect a total disregard for the integral value of the person we purport to love. If, in major ways, they are not what we think they should be, then perhaps it is better to allow them that dignity and coexist with them. We can at least accommodate and cooperate. But this requires real maturity. It will never happen if we are certain that we are always right, that the fault lies always with the other person. We can *help* others to change but only *they* can change.

Don't Blame Your Unhappiness Upon Others

We are totally responsible for ourselves. We cannot look for reasons outside of us. Still, we are forever blaming outside forces for our feelings and actions, seldom asking, "Why am I choosing to act or react that way?" Happiness and true freedom come only when we assume full responsibility for who and what we are. As long as we feel comfortable putting blame on others, we will never be required to evaluate and change our own behaviors. We blame parents for lack of love, response, nurturing. We blame society for keeping us from total freedom. We blame friends, lovers, teachers, even life. As long as we can pass the blame, we feel no necessity to change our own lives. After all, we are victims. There are those who even blame God for their misfortune and unhappiness. I have heard people say "I'll never forgive God for doing that to me!" What egos! These individuals see themselves helpless and hopeless and a part of an existence in which they have no control. They comfortably sit back in self-pity — waiting for lovers, family or God to "put it all right" for them. Sadly, many of them waste a valuable lifetime waiting!

Relationships are not dumping grounds for our selfishness, egocentricity, despair and anger. We only grow when we assume responsibility for our own joy and happiness. These cannot be generated from outside of us. Lasting happiness and peace come from within. When they are ours, then people and happenings come and go but joy remains ours forever. If it were not so then we could buy lasting joy. Having sufficient money to afford the things which bring us happiness or which enlarge our creative options for happiness, means a great deal. But it is not everything. My entire childhood was lived slightly above poverty level. Still I can hardly recall a more joyous time. With family packed into an old, beat-up Chevy, we started out on trips the car couldn't possibly make. But never mind, wherever we got was far enough for celebration. We laughed a lot. We found many reasons for merrymaking. We worked hard. We shared fully. We loved freely.

I received a letter from a woman dying of cancer. She commented that with this knowledge her whole family rallied about her as never before. (Isn't it interesting that we must die before others begin to treat us as human?) Freed of the mundane things she was previously required to do on a day-to-day basis, she decided to spend her last days getting acquainted with herself. She wrote: "I started to deal with the thoughts I think, the things I choose, the things I love, the books I read. I decided that these were a reflection of me and would tell me about myself. In so doing, I came to know a very fantastic person, *me*. The best thing that I learned after knowing I had to give up everything, was that all I really owned was what I was." She continued, "As I told you. I'm dying of cancer, but I have never been so alive and so happy!" Yes, one can be happy, even in impending death.

In selecting happiness over despair, we are able not only to generate it, but to make it contagious. All relationships are in great need of happiness. A life approached in joy can neutralize the all-too-present pain and apathy with which most people approach each day. And that is no small matter.

182

Be a Friend

So many of the responses to my relationship questionnaire stated that primary relationships were strengthened
when they began to include qualities they would nor-
mally reserve for secondary relationships, namely:
friendship. To be a friend to one's lover or members of
one's family may seem odd to some but is certainly a
wise insight, for friendship brings with it a keen desire to
know someone, the major requirement of love. It entails
a healthy curiosity directed away from ourselves — to
others in a noncompetitive, nonexploitive, non-
manipulative way. It is an unselfish desire to experience
other humans as they are and to bring them close enough
to allow them to tell us safely who they are.

It is strange that we are more prone to accept friends
and acquaintances for what they are than we are to accept
close loved ones. The more we care, the more we seem to
hurt, compare, and judge. In our zeal to make our loved
ones perfect or protect them from pain, we devalue them
as human beings. We are certainly not as trusting, toler-
ant or thoughtful with them as we are with friends. Still,
that is what is needed in loving each other.

Uta West, in her book, *If Love is the Answer, What is
the Question,* says that she believes . . . "that the trust
and tolerance and thoughtfulness that characterize
friendship at its best can heal and save all intimate
affiliations. Being a good friend — whether to yourself,
your mother, your child, or the person sharing your bed
— means first of all, respecting the integrity of the
individual."

I recall an interview I saw recently with a couple who

had managed to live lovingly together for 60 years. The husband, with a broad smile and a twinkle in his young eyes, volunteered, "She's been my best friend, as well as my lover!" Can there be a higher compliment?

Friendship reflects a deep regard for the value of the person. It tells us that people do not exist merely to satisfy our needs and fulfill our lives. They too have needs and lives to be actualized. In this sense we are responsible for ourselves while willingly accepting responsibility for another's becoming. It is a voluntary sharing, a mutual agreement to enrich each other's life processes through the revealing of ourselves as they do the same for us.

In a friendship, each individual affirms the other's presence and reinforces the other's integrity. As the friendship becomes deeper it becomes a sharing of vulnerabilities in a safe environment. We let each other know that our becoming is of the utmost interest and concern. We show in action that we respect and admire one another, that we enjoy the opportunity to be together and to share experiences.

The reader may wonder if this is not the definition of a deep loving relationship as well. The answer, of course, is "Yes, it is." The same dynamics involved in true friendship are those which are involved in love. Perhaps with the addition of such concepts as "more intimacy," "deeper," "most." In love we become *more* deeply involved in the other, *more* vulnerable, *more* responsible. We set aside *more* time to be close, to be intimate in mind as well as body, to communicate even the *most* private selves we know. We spend *more* time in willingly

184

enriching each other's lives, in sharing, in affirming and reinforcing.

We learn that we become most completely ourselves when we are most lost in another.

Don't Forget Rituals and Traditions

There are peoples and cultures in the world rich in tradition. They are the first to attest to the fact that their traditions have been mainly responsible for keeping them together, maintaining for them a sense of self as well as togetherness and offering them the dignity and strength to face tomorrow.

It has become popular these days to devalue tradition as romantic, ritualistic nonsense having little or no value to the present. We have discontinued wakes, Sunday family dinners, holiday get-togethers, the very human happenings which in the past bound us together in memory. In so doing, we have lost our sense of history. "Do you remember the day when _____?" Is that not cause enough for celebration? The old song revived. The note scratched on the back of a postcard, reread. The cake commemorating another year of life. The public renewal of marriage vows. Families who assemble at the graveside of dead members on their birthdays and assure each other that none of them will be forgotten, that love remembered is a part of each of them which makes them eternal.

My family celebrated everything: birthdays, holidays, Saint's days, sad times, happy times, anything which would bring the family together. My mother kept a calendar from which you could select almost any day as one for celebration! Every day, after all, is someone's birthday! We had traditional foods on designated days: risotto on Sundays, polenta on Fridays. There was the soup pot continually cooking on the stove, setting the air alive with a savory aroma changing according to leftovers which were added — pasta one day, peas and carrots the next, some chicken or beef the next. Whether the soup was thick or thin was determined upon Papa's income that week, Mama's shopping and the degree of leftovers. The time was always right for our warm bowl of soup. I can taste it still!

Was there a greater ritual than bagna calda? Here, gathered over a steaming pot of olive oil, garlic, herbs and sardines, we communally dunked crisp vegetables, catching the delectable drippings on crisp Italian bread and laughed and talked and stuffed our faces.

A *ritual* is defined as an established form of ceremony. A *tradition* is defined as the handing down of information, beliefs and customs by word of mouth or by example from one generation to another. These are things which bind and bond us, they are valued bonds that make working toward and facing tomorrow meaningful. As they are passed along from one generation to another, they always remain something certain, in a world of uncertainty. They offer an easily understood meaning to what might otherwise seem senseless.

Share Your Hopes and Dreams

Dreams elevate us beyond the mundane. They enrich our future with possibility. To dream together adds an element of wonder to our relationships and gives us something to look forward to. We dream of tomorrow's successes, of the children we desire, of the recognition we need, the travel we plan, of monetary security we hope for. We dream of peace, of pleasure, of joy. We must be careful, though, that we do not become so attached to these dreams that when they fail to materialize they shatter our belief in life. As long as the trip to Hawaii or Switzerland or Bangkok or Tokyo can always be put off, without trauma, the sustained idea may one day make these trips a reality. There is a joy in the planning, even if the dream is unrealized.

I recall that one of my dreams since childhood was to hear a crystal clear temple bell in a mountain monastery in Nepal. I was a product of mystical Lost Horizons and idyllic Shangri-las. Many thought that for a boy from East Los Angeles, this was truly a "pipe dream." Yet, there was something in me that knew that it would happen. I had only to concentrate and believe in the dream. It took years for the appropriate time but the sound of the bell was none the less clear and magical for having been dreamed about for so many years!

We all have hopes. Some of us see these as impossible and keep them to ourselves. We are certain that people will laugh or call us mad if we express them. How surprised we are that when we do share our hopes with others they eagerly tell of equally anticipated dreams. A dream is a private place and there is something special about sharing private places with those we love. It is one more way of allowing ourselves to be known.

You Will Need Courage

There can be no relationship in weakness. Timidity, uncertainty, fear of risk prevent us from coming together.

Relationships require us to be bold, to assert, to commit. Problems in human interaction are inevitable. There is no such thing as a perfect relationship which is utterly secure, happy and binding. By the very nature of a relationship, this cannot be. How can we expect that others will desire to be always with us? How do we expect to find someone who always will find happiness in the same things in which we find happiness, care about the same people, have the same interests or want to be doing the same activities at the same time? We can only realize this with robots and they make cold bed-fellows. By the very nature that relationships require two or more, there will always be differences. When we form a relationship we must give up the desire of the perfect resolution. Disagreements and frustrations are inevitable. Some we will solve. Others will seem unsolvable at the moment but we will overcome them in time. Others may, indeed, be insurmountable. "The problem is not that there are problems," says Dr. Theodore Rubin in *One to One,* "the problem is expecting otherwise and thinking that having problems is a problem."

We need courage to meet what comes and know that whatever it is, *it will not last forever.* Nothing lasts forever. Not pain, not joy, not even life. We need to accept the fact that the only way anything will ever be accomplished *exactly* as we want it, is if we do it. So if we choose to delegate, then it is natural that the results will vary in some way from what we intended and we must learn to accept it. If we have enough strength to take full responsibility for our failures as well as our successes then our self-respect is nurtured and grows. When we join others for mutual strength and support we will have to develop the courage of coexistence.

"The important thing is to be able at any moment to sacrifice what we are for what we could become."

- Charles Dubois

It's up to us to give our relationships a chance. There is nothing greater in life than loving another and being loved in return, for loving is the ultimate of experiences.

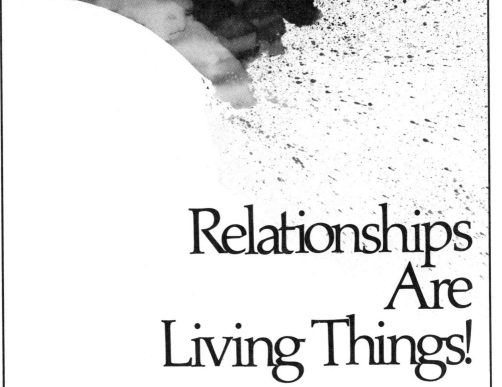

CHAPTER 10

Relationships
Are
Living Things!

Everything that lives
Lives not alone
Nor for itself.

WILLIAM BLAKE

Human survival is dependent upon healthy relating. The complex, ongoing process of people interacting with others in harmony, through each stage of life, is the highest and most demanding form of human behavior. David Viscott tells us:

> Relationships seldom die because they suddenly have no life left in them. They wither slowly, either because people do not understand how much or what kind of upkeep, time, work, love and caring they require or because people are too lazy or afraid to try. A relationship is a living thing. It needs and benefits from the same attention to detail that an artist lavishes on his art.

To fully understand relating, we must become both scientists and artists. As scientists we must isolate the components and qualities of a relationship into their separate parts (as has been attempted in the previous chapters). Then, we must analyze and study each part independently and concern ourselves with how they interrelate. As artists, we must view each of our relationships as creative challenges which will demand our deepest enthusiasm and boldest risk. We will be required to engage ourselves as scientists and artists in seeking deeply and analytically into ourselves (for we can know and understand others only to the degree to which we know and understand ourselves). At the same time we must extend ourselves toward our outer limits of talent and activity. We will need endless courage, persistence, will and effort: The courage to overcome attitudinal differences, remain flexible and hold to faith; the strength to face the reality of our aloneness; the persistence to meet failures and disappointment as we try again and again without guarantee; the effort to work at the development of skills required of relating as an ever-demanding, ever-changing process.

Though relationships seem to have an instinctive nature, experience has shown that we cannot depend upon it. It would be simpler if we could rely upon instinct rather than assume the arduous task and responsibility for creating and maintaining relationships. We must accept the fact that though our instincts to reach out to others in dependence can be traced to our infancy, beyond these basic biological motions we have pitifully few concrete skills for maintaining these relationships as we grow. Instinct plays but a small part in adult relating. As we mature we become more deeply aware of the devastating effects arising from aloneness. We yearn for the many rewards which come to us through moving toward others. But without growing knowledge, we lack the skills to come together in love. So, we continue to tumble through one painful situation after another, emerging with deep unhealing wounds, little new knowledge or sophistication, more cautious, less vulnerable and more frightened about trusting again.

Others of us would put the success of our relationship into the hands of love. With only a vague and romantic concept of what love means, we wait for love to do it all.

We want to believe that love solves all interpersonal problems, dilutes all differences, dissolves fears and anger, resolves all conflicts and, surrounding us with strength and warmth, will bring us to eternal bliss. This, like waiting for our instincts to guide us, has proved no more satisfactory a solution. In fact, placing ourselves in the hands of love has proved more of a problem than a solution. Having loved and lost, most of us have become suspicious of love. Too often we have reached out in what we believed to be love, only to recoil in awe at its power to collect tyrants and cause pain. Even where love is perfect it still is not a total solution to relationship.

To complicate matters, most of us have been raised to believe that strength lies in independence. Society tells us that we must make our own way. We come to believe that only when we no longer depend upon others can we say we have reached full maturity. We see *need* as immature and *dependence* as weakness. We fear commitment in that it may destroy our individuality and our much coveted freedom. In so feeling, we build self-imposed barriers to genuine encounter and the deep unions we so desperately seek. This is, indeed, a curious paradox. Deeply committed to freedom, liberation and independence on the one hand, and a deep need for togetherness on the other, we strive to unite in love. Such counterproductive belief and need systems only create more complex problems which, in the end, leave us frustrated, empty and unexplained.

It is true that we are all alone. This knowledge is devastating to many of us. Still, it is a fact. We are brought into the world alone and we will, no matter how many people love us, have to die alone. In between, we will have to grow alone, make personal decisions alone and determine our choices for change and growth, alone. Most of us feel this mounting sense of aloneness all of our lives.

In the book *Pairing,* Bach and Deutsch describe this in a most poignant manner. They say,

> By the millions, men and women yearn for intimate love and cannot find it . . . . night after night, day after day, they stalk one another, at once both hunters and the hunted. They prowl the singles bars and clubs and hotels, and cruises and weekend trips . . . . Robed and groomed and scented for the ritual, the brasher ones reach out, and the quiet ones watch and dream and wait. Then, with rare exception, everyone goes home, if not empty-handed, at least empty-hearted . . . . Others have lives that are filled, even overcrowded with people, or perhaps devoted to one important person they see regularly, sleep or live with. Yet most of them, too, have an inner sense of isolation . . . Why, they wonder, do they feel alone? Why does the old restlessness persist?

Love and relating help to make the knowledge of aloneness more bearable. The arms of a mother enfolding the newborn infant lessens the impact of birth trauma as does the warm hand touching ours later in life which gives us the necessary courage to accept pain. Through growing self-disclosure in commitment to each other, we minimize our isolation.

So we must, at last, accept full responsibility for the success or failure of emerging from aloneness and our coming together in love. We cannot look to instincts or even count on deep love. The only hope lies in a serious study of our relationships. We must try to better know who we are, who the other is, and what dynamics are required to keep us united.

Our lives are intricate patterns of relationships in which our motivations, our desire, our beliefs, our needs and our dreams are intricately attached. To a large extent we can know and define ourselves as individuals by examining the patterns of our relationships. In our earliest relating with parents and siblings we had no choice. We depended upon these individuals because we, as human beings, required more intensive care for a longer period of dependency than any living creature. But it is also true that we humans are among those who have the longest life span. So, over the years, we find that we are required to adapt to different types of relationships in order to fill new complex physical, social and emotional needs for nurturance, for companionship, for sexuality, for security, for status, for growth.

So to bring another into our life in love we must be willing to give up certain destructive characteristics. For example:

The need to be always right.

The need to be first in everything.

The need to be constantly in control.

The need to be perfect.

The need to be loved by everyone.

The need to possess.

The need to be free of conflict and frustration.

The need to change others for our needs.

The need to manipulate.

The need to blame.

The need to dominate.

It is not surprising that even the healthiest among us has relating problems. When two or more individuals move toward each other, even willfully and in love, the processes which will bring them together and keep them together will be monumentally complex. Balance and security will be shaken. New behaviors and changes will be required. Depending upon our level of experience, ability to adjust, our needs, we will respond differently to these demands.

There are several strategies we can use to deal with these problems.

We can deny that they exist.

We can acknowledge their existence but avoid doing anything about them.

We can harden ourselves against them and live with them.

We can view them as irreversible and terminate the relationship.

Or:

We can take them on as a challenge from which we may profit, realizing that, over time, the more we have learned about problem-solving in relating, the greater will be our ability to love each other.

It is hoped that most of us will accept the last possibility.

ANNOTATED BIBLIOGRAPHY

We become, in a sense, a part of all that we perceive. People, environments and experiences become so much a part of us that we fail to realize their special role in our thoughts and behavior.

Among many other experiences, the following books have, over the past few years, changed my way of seeing the world and interacting in it. I present them here for those who desire to continue to grow with me in understanding and love.

Albee, Edward: *The American Dream*. New York: Coward-McCann, Inc., 1960.
> A pseudo-comedy which deals with artificial values and behaviors in our society.

Augsburger, David: *Caring Enough to Forgive: True Forgiveness/Caring Enough to Not Forgive: False Forgiveness*. Ventura, California: Regal Books, 1981.
> A definitive, wise and highly recommended work on forgiveness. It deals forcefully with issues of wrongdoing, reaffirmation, releasing past hurt, repentance and coming together in peace and love.

Augsburger, David: *The Freedom of Forgiveness*. Chicago, Illinois: Moody Press, 1973.
> This, with David Augsburger's other book form the basis of the best work I've read on the dynamics and how-to of forgiveness.

Bach, George and Deutsch, Ronald: *Pairing*. New York: Avon Books, 1970.

A fine work on the subtle art of moving together with others.

Beecher, Marguerite and Willard: *The Mark of Cain*. New York: Harper and Row, 1971.

A thoughtful and important book on jealousy — its meaning and its effect.

Berne, Eric: *Games People Play*. New York: Grove Press, 1964.

The master work on transactional analysis (transpersonal psychology). A revealing discussion of the games people play and why and how they play them.

Bernstein, Leonard: *Candide*. New York: Amberson Enterprises, Inc., 1976.

A comic operetta based upon Voltaire's satire. In a creative, outrageous way it deals with human foolishness, adjustability, survival, relationships and love. A delight!

Bloomfield, Harold and Felder, Leonard: *Making Peace With Your Parents*. New York: Random House, 1983.

A very readable work on the rebuilding of bridges with those we love.

Branden, Nathaniel: *The Psychology of Romantic Love*. New York: J.P. Tarcher, Inc. (Distributed by St. Martin's Press, Inc.), 1980.

A much praised and recognized work of the complex subject of why and how we "fall in love" and some stimulating ideas for making love work.

Bresler, Dr. David with Richard Trubo: *Free Yourself From Pain*. New York: Simon and Schuster, 1979.

An interesting book by an expert on stress and pain in which he helps us to learn ways of healing ourselves.

Bristol, Goldie with Carol McGinnis: *When It's Hard To Forgive*. Wheaton, Illinois: Victor Books, 1982.

The dramatic story of a couple who were faced with the terrible pain of loss and found their redemption in forgiveness.

Buber, Martin: *I and Thou*. New York: Scribner, 1970.

A rather difficult work which deals with the values of loving communication as well as sound messages of living life with high spirituality and love.

Clanton, Gordon and Lynn G. Smith: *Jealousy*. Englewood Cliffs, New Jersey: Prentice Hall, Inc., 1977.

A rare experience for those concerned with what jealousy is and what causes it, the good and bad of being jealous and what can be done about it.

Colton, Helen: *The Gift of Touch: How Physical Contact Improves Communication, Pleasure and Health*. New York: Putnam Publishing Group, 1983.

Helen Colton has become one of the leading experts and exponents of creating togetherness through touching.

Cousins, Norman: *Human Options*. New York: Berkley Books, 1981.

Selections of the author's writings for the Saturday Review deals with education, survival, learning, creativity, healing and freedom.

Dunn, David: *Try Giving Yourself Away*. Englewood Cliffs, New Jersey: Prentice Hall, Inc., 1970.

A practical guide to sharing yourself with others in a more broadened and enriched manner — conducive to the growth of all parties involved.

Faulkner, William: *Essays, Speeches, and Public Lectures*. New York: Random House, Inc., 1965.

Reference.

Fromme, Allan: *The Ability to Love*. North Hollywood, California: Wilshire Book Company, 1965.

An interesting work on the human expression of loving — how it is created and manifested in daily life.

Gould, Roger: *Transformations*. New York: Simon and Schuster, 1978.

An excellent work dealing with the changes which the person undergoes from birth, childhood, marriage, creative adulthood to death. It stresses the value of mourning and discomfort as we take leave of childhood needs and move toward maturity.

Humphrey, Nicholas: The Bronowski Memorial Lectures, "Four Minutes to Midnight." *The Listener,* October 29, 1981. BBC Publications, Marylebone, High Street, London.

Reference.

Hyers, Conrad: *Zen and the Comic Spirit*. Philadelphia, Pennsylvania: Westminster Press, 1973.

One of the few and excellent studies of joy, laughter and the comic spirit.

Jampolsky, Gerald: *Love is Letting Go of Fear*. Berkeley, California: Celestial Arts, 1979.

A small book based upon the author's course in Miracles which helps us to understand that fear keeps us from love. Suggested ways of letting go of fear to allow love to enter are presented for the reader.

Liebman, Joshua Loth: *Hope for Man*. New York: Simon and Schuster, 1966.

A highly optimistic work which embraces life and its challenges. It addresses love, courage, happiness and maturity in inner security.

Lindbergh, Anne Morrow: *Gift From the Sea*. New York: Pantheon Book, Inc., 1955.

A classic work about the liberation of the mind and spirit using the author's experience with the sea as the great metaphor.

Lyon, Harold: *Tenderness is Strength*. New York: Harper and Row, 1977.

A wonderful book that offers many insights into loving, risking, and growing. Readable, enjoyable and helpful.

May, Rollo: *Love and Will*. New York: W.W. Norton and Co., 1969.

A classic available to those of us who are interested in the dynamics of human love.

Mead, Margaret: *Coming of Age in Samoa*. New York: William Morrow & Company, 1971.

For general investigation at the roots of culture and human behavior. Has been criticized of late by anthropologists but it is nonetheless valuable.

Merton, Thomas: *Love and Living*. New York: Bantam Publishing, 1980.

One of Merton's most interesting books published ten years after his death. He deals with intriguing subjects such as learning to live, to be aware, to appreciate solitude and to understand death, Christian humanities and love.

Mindess, Harvey: *Laughter and Liberation*. Los Angeles, California: Nash Publications, 1971.

A superb work on the liberating effect of humor and laughter.

Montagu, Ashley and Floyd Matson: *The Human Connection*. New York: McGraw-Hill, 1979.

A classic in the field of human communication. It looks deeply into how we approach each other, touch and interact. They offer us many insights into love and loving — which they refer to as "the ultimate human connection."

Montagu, Ashley: *Touching: The Human Significance of the Skin*. New York: Columbia University Press, 1971.

One of the definitive works on touching. Here, Montagu, the anthropologist and humanitarian, explains touching as a basic need for growth and survival.

Moody, Dr. Raymond: *Laugh After Laugh*. Stanton, Virginia: Headwaters Press, 1978.

> One of the rare works on the "Healing Power of Humor." It looks at the relationship of humor to questions of health and disease. Though an M.D., Dr. Moody criticizes his own profession for overlooking the God-given ability to help the healing process through a good laugh and a sense of humor.

Morris, Desmond: *Intimate Behaviors*. New York: Random House, 1971.

> A superb book. Highly recommended and readable. Morris deals with intimacy through its many facets and how they relate to human behavior.

Moustakas, Clark: *Creative Life*. New York: Van Nostrand Reinhold Co., 1977.

> A beautifully written book on the joy of the creative, fully realized life.

Piaget, Jean: *The Moral Judgement of the Child*. New York: Free Press, 1966.

> Reference.

Rogers, Carl: *Becoming Partners: Marriage and Its Alternatives*. New York: Delacorte Press, 1973.

> A very readable excellent work by one of our most human psychologists. It looks deeply and perceptively into modern marriage and its alternatives.

Roosevelt, Eleanor: *You Learn By Living*. Philadelphia, Pennsylvania: Westminster Press, 1983.

> A very human, wise and valuable look at life and love by a most perceptive, caring woman.

Rubin, Theodore Issac: *Compassion and Self Hate*. New York: McKay Company, Inc., 1975.

> A most thoughtful work by a caring psychiatrist which challenges us to give up dreams of perfection, degrading behaviors and being our own worst enemy.

204

Rubin, Theodore Isaac: *Reconciliation.* New York: The Viking Press, Inc., 1980.

Psychiatrist Theodore Rubin writes of the self-destructive style of life that many of us engage in and recommends a type of "tranquil aliveness" in its place. He deals with relationships in terms of when to preserve them and when they need to be ended. He suggests ways in which we may find inner peace.

Rubin, Theodore Isaac: *One to One.* New York: The Viking Press, Inc., 1983.

A very fine work on the subtle art of relationships — how to deal and grow with them.

Schoenfeld, Eugene, MD: *Jealousy, Taming the Green-Eyed Monster.* New York: Holt, Rinehart and Winston, 1979.

A perceptive look at jealousy from childhood to adulthood — how it is programmed and the effect it has upon the person. It also includes methods of coping with jealousy — both temporary and lasting.

Swanson, Donna: *Mind Song.* Nashville, Tennessee: Upper Room, 1978.

A group of readable and meaningful poems which deal with life, love and living.

Viscott, David: *How to Live with Another Person.* New York: Arbor House, 1974.

One of the most practical guides to living with another person in peace and love.

Viscott, David: *Risking.* New York: Simon and Schuster, 1977.

A common sense approach to living with risk. Psychiatrist Viscott helps the reader to take risks without fear. It offers ways in which we seize the unknown with a feeling of adventure rather than worry.

Watson, Lillian: *Light From Many Lamps.* New York: Simon and Schuster, 1951.

A collected work of inspirational essays by some of the world's fine human beings and philosophers.

West, Uta: *If Love is the Answer, What is the Question?* New York: McGraw-Hill, 1977.

An easy-to-read, clever but not superficial look at love.

Wolk, Robert L. and Henley, Arthur: *The Right to Lie.* New York: Peter H. Wyden, Inc., 1970.

An interesting and thought-provoking look at lying.

Wyse, Lois: *Lovetalk.* Garden City, New York: Doubleday, 1973.

Lovetalk is subtitled "How to say what you mean to someone you love." It is a superb collection of poems which deal with our inability to express love and explain our deepest feelings. It is dedicated to giving us insights into the loving life.

For additional reading on these subjects, please also see the Bibliography at the end of my book *Personhood.*

ACKNOWLEDGMENTS

We are pleased to acknowledge permission to reprint brief quotations from the following works.

David Augsburger. *Caring Enough to Not Forgive*. Ventura: Regal Books, © 1981.

Marguerite and Willard Beecher. *The Mark of Cain*. New York: Harper and Row, © 1971.

David Bresler. *Free Yourself From Pain*. New York: Simon & Schuster, © 1979.

Goldie Bristol and Carol McGinnis. *When It's Hard to Forgive*. Wheaton: Victor Books, © 1982.

Helen Colton. *The Gift of Touch: How Physical Contact Improves Communication, Pleasure and Health*. New York: Putnam Group Publishing, © 1983.

William Faulkner. *Essays, Speeches and Public Lectures*. New York: Random House, © 1965.

Allan Fromme. *The Ability to Love*. New York: Farrar, Straus & Giroux.

Roger L. Gould. *Transformations*. New York: Simon & Schuster, © 1978.

Joshua Loth Liebman. *Hope to Man*. New York: Simon & Schuster, © 1966.

Anne Morrow Lindbergh. *Gift From the Sea*. New York: Random House, © 1955, © 1975 by the author.

Harold Lyon. *Tenderness Is Strength*. New York: Harper and Row, © 1977.

Rollo May. *Love and Will*. New York: WW Norton and Company, © 1969.

Ashley Montagu & Floyd Matson. *Human Connections*. New York: McGraw-Hill, © 1979.

Desmond Morris. *Intimate Behavior*. New York: Random House, © 1971.

Clark Moustakas. *Creative Life*. New York: Van Nostrand Reinhold Company, © 1977.

Theodore Rubin. *One to One*. New York: Viking Press © 1983.

Donna Swanson. *Mind Song*. Nashville: Upper Room, © 1978.

David Viscott. *How to Live with Another Person*. New York: Arbor House Publishing Company, © 1974.

Robert Wolk. *The Right to Lie*. New York: The David McKay Co., © 1970.

Lois Wyse. *Lovetalk*. New York: Doubleday, © 1973.